A Spiritual Journey
Into the Future

Ewert H. Cousins

Preface by
Robley E. Whitson

Edited and
Introduction by
Janet Kvamme Cousins

A Spiritual Journey
Into the Future

by Ewert H. Cousins

Copyright © 2010

ISBN 1-55605-425-4
978-155605-425-9
Library of Congress Control Number: 2010941827

WYNDHAM HALL PRESS
5050 Kerr Rd
Lima, Ohio 45806
www.wyndhamhallpress.com

Printed in the United States of America

Table of Contents

Dedicated to Ewert Cousins' Son and Daughters
Hilary, Sara, Emily

Acknowledgements

To the people who contributed to the making of this book:

Dr. Robley Whitson, who first had the idea for this book and who has been a constant source of advice on its style and editing.

Dr. John Morgan, President of the Graduate Theological Foundation, who was willing to support this project and to publish it.

Ashley Young and **Nik Elevitch**, for their generosity in typing and formatting. Their contribution was invaluable.

Maureen McCurdy, who typed an additional essay.

Dave Cedarholm, who painstakingly proofread the text.

Permission has been generously granted to use material published in the following chapters:

1. Mysticism and the Spiritual Journey
In *Studies in Formative Spirituality. Journal of Ongoing Formation*. 5:1 (Feb., 1984): pp. 11-20.

2. Bernard of Clairvaux and The Spiritual Path of Love:
         A Global Phenomenon
This is the preface to *Bernard of Clairvaux: Selected Works*. Translation and foreword by G. R. Evans, Introduction by Jean Leclerq, O.S.B. Preface by Ewert H. Cousins. Copyright c. 1987 by Gillian R. Evans. *Classics of Western Spirituality* (New York, Mahwah, N. J.: Paulist Press, 1987), pp. 5-11. Reprinted by permission of Paulist Press, Inc. www.paulistpress.com

3. 4. Franciscan Roots of Ignatian Meditation
In *Ignatian Spirituality in a Secular Age*, George P. Schner, ed. Papers presented at a symposium, Regis College March 20-21 (Waterloo, Ontario: Wilfred Laurier University Press, 1984), pp. 51-64. Reprinted by permission of Wilfrid Laurier University Press. www.wlupress.wlu.ca

5. The Mysticism of the Historical Event
In *Mysticism and Religious Traditions*. Steven T. Katz, ed. (New York, Oxford: Oxford University Press 1983), pp. 166-169. Reprinted by permission of Oxford University Press. www.oup.com

6. The *Coincidentia Oppositorum* in the Theology of Bonaventure
First published in French in *etudes franciscaines*, tome 18, supplement annuel (1968): 15-31. Actes du Colloque Saint Bonaventure. 9-12 septembre (1968) English version in *The Cord*, (1970): 260-269, 307-314. Reprinted by permission of *The Cord*. www.franciscanpublications.sbu.edu

7. Francis of Assisi and Interreligious Dialogue
In New Ecumenical Research Association, Seventh International Conference on "God: The Contemporary Discussion," Cittadella Ospitalia, Assisi, Italy, May 1-7, 1990. Published in *Dialogue and Alliance*, 5:2 (1990): 20-23. Reprinted by permission of *Dialog and Alliance*.

8. Cross Cultural Research: Hindu and Christian
In *Salzburg Studies in English Literature*, directed by Erwin A. Stürzl. *Elizabethan & Renaissance Studies*, ed. James Hogg. (92) 20. This volume, *Mysticism: Medieval & Modern*, ed. Valerie M. Lagorio. Institut Für Anglistik Und Amerikanistik. Universität Salzburg. Salzburg, Austria, 1986. Original article title "Transcultural Phenomenology and Meister Eckhart." pp. 101-1

9. 10. States of Consciousness: Charting the Mystical Path
In The Fires of Desire: Erotic Energies and the Spiritual Quest, eds. Frederica P. Halligan and and John J. Shea (New York: Crossroad, 1992), pp. 126-141. Reprinted by permission of the editors.

11. Interreligious Dialogue and the Future of Hermeneutics
Estratto from *Archivio di Filosofia*, dir. Marco M. Olivetti (Roma: Istituto di Studi Filosofici, 1980), pp. 93-102.

12. My Journey Into Interreligious Dialogue, with Janet Cousins.
A two-part article in *Monastic Interreligious Dialogue Bulletin*. 73 (October 2004): 18-24. 74 (April 2005) 18-24. Published on the web. Reprinted by permission of MID. www.monasticdialog.com

13. Global Spirituality
In Philip Sheldrake, ed. *The New Westminster Dictionary of Christian Spirituality* (Louisville, KY: Westminster John Knox Press, 2005) pp. 321-323. Reprinted by permission of Westminster John Knox Press. www.wjkbooks.com

14. Religions of the World Facing the Future Together
This article has reappeared under several different titles. It was first published as "Judaism—Christianity—Islam: Facing Modernity Together" *Journal of Ecumenical Studies* 30: 3-4 (Summer-Fall 1993): 417-25; as "The Convergence of Cultures a nd Religions in Light of the Evolution of Consciousness" *Zygon: Journal of Religion and Science* 34:2 (June 1999): 209-219; as "Religions of the World: Facing Modernity Together" *Global Virtue Ethics Review* 1:1 (1999): 8-20; as "Religions of the World: Teilhard and the Second Axial Turning" *Interreligious Insight* 4:4 (October 2006): 8-19. Reprinted by permission of the *Journal of Ecumenical Studies*. www.journal.jesdialogue.org

I believe, then, that the mystic's experience manifests in an intense often dramatic fashion the dynamics and structures of experience encountered by the majority of those on a spiritual journey.

In our era, with increasing communication and with the convergence of cultures, we are beginning to awaken to the fact that we have been on a single spiritual journey from the very outset.

Ewert H. Cousins

A Spiritual Journey Into the Future
Preface

The chapters of this study were published separately as Ewert Cousins explored various dimensions of the contemporary religions quest. He sought to test ideas and context and thus gain insight through the feedback from fellow scholars, and monastic and other spiritual guides, and religious leaders of the different traditions. It was always an open ended process as he was convinced we are entering a new era of unitive spiritual development. Every question asked could only receive a partial and provisional answer in light of an emerging new sense of experience as both personal and interpersonal, as individual and communal: a new kind of human consciousness.

One of his basic insights is the necessity to re-explore our religious past—or, perhaps better, our religious pasts—not only as history but as demonstrations of a long and complex developmental process not at all a smooth continuum. His study of medieval Christian mysticism, especially as formulated in neo-Platonic logos-theology, led him to recognize comparable movements in other traditions of roughly the same period, especially Sufi mysticism among Muslims, the bhakti divine love principle in Hinduism, and the Compassionate Amida Buddha of Pure Land Buddhism.

Paralleling Cousins' awareness of the multiple paths of the spiritual journey in personal/individual mysticism, is that of the new vision of our cosmos unveiled by modern science and of our human world paradoxically in a crisis of survival and yet also at a moment of great creative potential. This vision for the present-to-future centers on the call for a new kind of plural-unitive community now possible because of the new social reality of global consciousness.

Dr. Robley E. Whitson
Graduate Theological Foundation

Introduction

In this book Ewert Cousins has spanned the distance from the spiritual journey of the individual soul to the coming together and spiritual journey of the world's religions. Yet he never loses sight of the need for being grounded in one's own tradition while being open to dialogue with and urgent planetary intervention with other spiritual communities.

Cousins' medieval mentors were Francis and Bonaventure and his strong modern influences were Teilhard de Chardin and Jung. He begins with the soul's journey into God, and the classical formulation of purgation, illumination, and union. In the deft strokes of a master he shows us that the ecstatic experience of the mystics can guide us in our own experience and spiritual path. Further, he offers some of the various maps of the spiritual journey. Not only does he know these paths through academic study, but as often has been noted, his knowledge comes from experience. This coupled with solid scholarly knowledge is a constant feature of the themes of this book and of his life.

The spiritual path of love—the soul as lover and God as the beloved, most notably in the *Song of Songs* as portrayed in Bernard of Clairvaux, is "not confined to Christianity in twelfth-century France." In that century, "in various traditions and in diverse geographical areas, love was cultivated as a spiritual path with an intensity and a creativity that was unprecedented." It is a surprising global phenomenon which Cousins discovered in the course of his travels related to interreligious publishing.

Underlying Cousins' ability to penetrate into the deeper meaning of the writing of Bernard is his own experience as a leading medievalist and Bonaventure scholar and thus his familiarity with the four-fold sense of scripture which illumines the allegorical significance of the *Song of Songs* for Bernard. Further, Cousins' personal preference was for the four-fold sense of scripture as defined by Dante, in which the literal sense was the background for the higher sense in the allegorical.

Colleagues and students were often struck by Cousins' penchant for the paradoxical, and his presentation here of the unexpected combination of Franciscan roots of Ignatian meditation is a case in point. In the classical scholastic style, Cousins first presents the opposing points of view, showing the obvious differences between the free spirited Francis and the methodological Ignatius. Then he demonstrates the historical and amply documented instances of meditation on the life of Christ in the thirteenth century Francis and the early Franciscan tradition. But Cousins is not limited to the historical, he also explores the psychological, spiritual, and theological. This is characteristic of the breadth of Cousins' approach to a topic.

While Francis at Greccio made the audience actors in the birth of Christ, Bonaventure, as the "second founder of the Franciscan order," wrote a reflection on the nativity scene, drawing the reader into meditation on the story. Having read a later version of this nativity narrative, in Ignatius' meditation it becomes much more structured. Beyond his scholarship, Cousins is amply equipped to examine the contemplation on the life of Christ as the common core of both Franciscan and Ignatian spirituality. He spent thirteen years as a Jesuit, so he knows Jesuit spirituality from experience. Later he became closely aligned with the Franciscans, particularly in his role as one of the world leaders in the Bonaventure Centennial, his translation of several of Bonaventure's works, and his book on Bonaventure.

Coming from the devotion to the life of Christ, is a form of mysticism which Cousins has personally identified as "a distinctive form of mystical consciousness." He calls this "the mysticism of the historical event." One imagines the scene and the historical characters and enters into the drama and is psychologically and spiritually "there." This is the type of prayer used by both Francis and Ignatius.

Cousins' essay on the *coincidentia oppositorum* in Bonaventure was pivotal in his becoming recognized as one of the world's leading Bonaventure scholars. Cousins saw the coincidence of opposites as an ancient symbol, particularly in the East. But it had fallen out of discourse in the West since its deliberate usage by Nicholas of Cusa in the sixteenth century. It was Cousins who brought it back into theological language. It may seem from the chapter that he is crediting Mircea Eliade with this achievement. However, a careful reading reveals that although Eliade, in his description of hierophany is using a related term, he does not name the notion of the coincidence of opposites. Since Cousins used this ancient concept in his chapter on *coincidentia oppositorum* and in later in his book, *Bonaventure and the Coincidence of Opposites*, it has appeared in theological articles by others.

The "coincidence of opposites" is an idea which permeates Cousins' thinking. He categorically states that "the proper theoretical model for studying Bonaventure's thought is that of the *coincidentia oppositorum*." In Cousins' analysis of Bonaventure, "Christ unites within himself the greatest possible coincidence of opposites." Thus, the idea of the "coincidence of opposites" is intrinsic to Bonaventure's concept of the divine. Cousins finds in Bonaventure the same point of view that he himself holds. Thus, the "coincidence of opposites" is also intrinsic to Cousins' concept of the divine. Opposites, in this sense, are held together in tension. As Cousins writes of Bonaventure,

"Christ himself is the greatest coincidence of opposites, who integrates in himself all opposites and draws them to their completion and ultimate reconciliation."

The notion of "coincidence of opposites" has served Cousins well in his contacts with persons of other traditions. He saw complementary aspects in, for instance, Islam and Christianity. In Islam the emphasis is placed on God as transcendent. In Christianity the immanence of incarnation is clearly prominent.

As Cousins states in the beginning of his chapter on Francis of Assisi and interreligious dialogue, "It is especially meaningful for me to speak here in Assisi on St. Francis and interreligious dialogue." He goes on to say that this occasion "marks the meeting of two major paths that I have taken in my academic and spiritual journeys." These journeys "have constantly intersected, even interpenetrated." This statement is true of both Cousins' life and his work. People who knew him in one area of expertise, for instance, Bonaventure and Franciscan studies, were amazed to discover that he was also a pioneer and leader in interreligious dialogue. Sandra Schneiders expresses this well: " . . . I was invited to join a group of scholars whom Dr. Cousins had convened to discuss the possibility of publishing a multi-volume encyclopedia of world spiritualities. I had always associated Ewert Cousins with the study of medieval theology and spirituality . . . But in that discussion I experienced first hand his broader and deeper concern, that is, his twofold passion to explore the rich particularity of the Christian tradition of spirituality and to engage responsibly the challenging universality of the spiritual quest across religious, ethnic, and chronological boundaries."[1]

Cousins has created a kind of allegory, in which key events in Francis' life symbolize some of the steps necessary for in-depth interreligious dialogue. Francis' stripping away and his nakedness before all symbolizes the temporary stripping away of one's own attitudes as a precursor to understanding the position of the other. This requires humility in the presence of the other. Cousins held this humility himself, deeply respecting the position of the other person as valid as his own. He, too, rejoiced in the varieties of religious consciousness as Francis rejoiced in the varieties of creatures.

Here again, from the perspective of the "coincidence of opposites" he urges us to "appropriate into our own worldview the richness we have discovered from dialogue with others."

A different kind of interreligious dialogue is described in Cousins' collaborative research with a Hindu scholar. Here two factors supply a background for this cross-cultural research project. Cousins held a doctorate in philosophy and he had participated over several years in a research seminar headed by Peter Berger, the sociologist of religion. This seminar investigated the experiences of mystics in the world's religions.

Cousins wanted a more detailed project. In India, he discovered that Professor Balasubramanian of the University of Madras, had been studying Hindu mysticism by using phenomenology, the same method that Cousins was using to study Christian mysticism. They did some comparative work on Eckhart and Sánkara, both of whom were negative theologians from these two world traditions. They planned further study using the positive theologians Bonaventure and Râmânuja. The introduction of phenomenology gave to their dialogue a methodology with several stages. The first was to "encounter mystical consciousness." The second is to "enter into the consciousness of the mystic," and the third to describe the contents of the consciousness of the mystic." Here he focused on the intentionality of the mystic, that is, of God mysticism, and on ontology, or the subject's intention to reach the reality of the divine. However, the phenomenological approach is not typical of Cousins work. He almost always used a metaphysical means of looking at mystical texts.

The mystical or spiritual path and the psyche or the erotic energies are the subject of a chapter on states of consciousness. It was first presented at a Jungian conference at Fordham University titled: "Fires of Desire: Erotic Energies and the Spiritual Quest."[2] Cousins often used a Jungian lens to look at spirituality. His talk met with overwhelming acclaim. He was not only qualified though his academic research to speak on spirituality, but he had a strong interest in psychotherapy, and was well versed in psychology. For some time he met with a group of psychotherapists headed by Rollo May to discuss psychological issues. Originally he had considered doing his doctorate in philosophy on interpersonal relations. However, he found what he was looking for in Richard of St. Victor and the relationship among the persons in the Trinity.

Cousins reserves the term mysticism for "the transcendent with an ecstatic or rapturous intensity of consciousness." He describes, often in their own words, the experiences of several saints who have reached a rapturous experience. Augustine cries out "O eternal truth, and true love and beloved eternity." Bernard of Clairvaux speaks of the passionate love of the Bride and the Bridegroom. Teresa of Avila describes the soul as an interior castle in the center of which, the soul is united to God in a mystical marriage.

In the work of Robert Masters and Jean Houston, and of Stanislav Grof, Cousins finds a blending of the parts of the psyche reached by mystical experience and that reached by psychotherapy. Yet he does not think this or any other model to be the ultimate in integrating spirituality and psychotherapy.

Rather, he proposes an integration of the two images of the psyche or soul coming from psychotherapy and spirituality.

Cousins introduced yet another element into interreligious dialogue—hermeneutics. He urges the transformation of Western hermeneutics to bring it into a global context. Cousins compares the "openness to experience and of pluralism" of the United States with the "self-reflective critical consciousness" of Europe and expresses the need for a combination of these positions. He could make this observation because for many years, he presented papers at what was popularly known as the "Castelli Conferences" in Italy where he came into contact with the leading European theologians. His paper, on interreligious dialogue and the future of hermeneutics" was presented at a Castelli Conference in Rome.

The influence of Bonaventure is evident in Cousins' description of the Father as the fountain fullness in the Trinity. In interreligious dialogue Cousins has previously proposed the temporary stripping away of one's own tradition. However, in this instance, he considers the dynamic image of the Trinity as a template for understanding the primordial or deep experience underlying the hermeneutics of the other. This may be explained by the fact that Cousins was impressed with the work of Raimundo Panikkar, who holds a Trinitarian construct of the world's major religions. The voice of Teilhard de Chardin is evident in such words as "complexified" or "planetized" consciousness. These sources have left their imprint upon Cousins' thought, but his use of them is distinctly his own.

When the editor of Monastic Interreligious Dialogue Bulletin was asked what writing of the eighty three issues he considered the most significant, his immediate response was Ewert Cousins,' "My Journey into Interreligious Dialogue."[3] This is a good story, beginning with cowboys and Indians in South Dakota and ending with the Himalayas. More importantly, it shows how at an early stage in Cousins' life, he opened himself to the mystical experience of Lakota culture and spirituality. His experience of temporarily letting go of his own culture and religious tradition and "passing over" into that of another tradition and "coming back" became the pattern for later excursions of "passing over" into other religious traditions and coming back. Years later he was to learn how in John Dunne, *The Way of All the Earth*, his own experience was described and named.[4] Among the most dramatic examples of this religious adventure was Cousins' visit to a mosque in Bethlehem. There he felt the overwhelming transcendence of God which the Muslims express in their deep bowing.

A colorful part of this chapter is the description of the interreligious conference at the United Nations in 1975. The drama of the liturgical events, the moving speech by Mother Teresa on the poor of India, and the meetings with eminent spiritual leaders all capture our imagination. But during all the drama, something else was happening within the mind of Cousins which was to determine his later direction. It was through the United Nations Conference that Cousins conceived the concept of the Second Axial Period. This insight will be discussed in detail later in this introduction.

Earlier we have described a chapter on the mysticism of the historical event. Cousins held another, related form of mysticism, the mysticism of the sacred place. He held, as do many, that certain places have a mystical quality about them, among them Assisi. Cousins respected the Buddhist tradition that the Himalayas, particularly Mount Everest, as we call it, is such a sacred place. High in the Himalayas two Buddhist monasteries, one in Tibet and the other in Nepal, were built just to contemplate "the Mother Goddess of the Earth" or the "Mother Goddess of the Sky" among other names. As Cousins says of the Himalayas, "they have a silent grandeur that hovers between earth and heaven and beckons the spiritual seeker to rise to realms of overwhelming majesty."

"Not many academicians can be credited with founding a new sub-discipline in their field, but with "world spirituality"—a phrase that joins breadth (the world) to depth (spirituality)—Ewert Cousins has done just that."[5] This was said by the noted explorer of the world religions, Huston Smith. Cousins' achievements in world or global spirituality are manifold. In publishing he was the chief editorial consultant of the 100 plus volume series *The Classics of Western Spirituality* and general editor of the 25-volume series *World Spirituality: An Encyclopedic History of the Religious Quest*. He coordinated numerous conferences on world spirituality, interreligious dialogue, including a conference of world religious leaders at the United Nations. He traveled extensively to research the world's religions. It is not surprising then, that when Philip Sheldrake was planning *The New Westminster Dictionary of Christian Spirituality*, he specifically wanted Cousins to write the article on "global spirituality."

One of Cousins' major contributions to religion and related fields, particularly interreligious dialogue and world/global spirituality, is his theory of the Second Axial Period. He takes the observation of Karl Jaspers that between 800 and 200 BC a transformation of consciousness occurred in three major geographical regions. Human consciousness shifted from tribal to individual identity, and in that shift. the great religions of the world came into being. Using Jaspers' notion as a starting point, Cousins constructed a completely new concept.

In recalling the genesis of this notion, he looked back to the 1975 interreligious conference at the United Nations, "One is the Human Spirit." ".

. . through the dynamics of the conference and its orientation towards the future, I gained my initial insight of the Second Axial Period . . . . A new form of consciousness was being born, and it required a new name, which I called the Second Axial Period."[6]

Just as the future orientation and the joining together of the religions and cultures at the United Nations conference had impressed Cousins; similarly, the futuristic evolution of humanity as set forth by Teilhard was compatible with the futuristic outlook of Cousins. Like Teilhard, he held that during the past century there had been a gradual change from divergence to convergence. This change, he said "is drawing various cultures into a single planetized community." He declared that to successfully accomplish this convergence, we need to reach back into the Pre-Axial notion of a single tribe connected to the earth and the universe, and with the spirituality of the First Axial Period integrate earthly and heavenly concerns.

Cousins considered the Second Axial Period to be so significant that he brought it into a number of his writings and oral presentations. In the final chapter, on the religions of the world facing the future together, he spells out in more detail his connectedness to Teilhard de Chardin. Teilhard had a strong influence, particularly in the formation of Cousins' theory. He found in Teilhard's paleethnological development of the human phenomena, parallels to his own observations. The religions of the world, he noted, are entering more and more into dialogue with each other. In this unity, the distinct character of each tradition is not lost, but intensified.

Cousins urges that we not only come together on a spiritual level but channel our spiritual energies into saving our planet. The imperative facing the religions of the world is together to solve the problems of the earth that threaten our existence.

Dr. Janet Kvamme Cousins, Editor

Chapter 1:
Mysticism and the Spiritual Journey

For more than a decade there has been widespread interest in both spirituality and mysticism. The spiritual journey has been pursued with vigor by spiritual seekers both within and without the established religious traditions. In addition spirituality and mysticism have become the object of academic study, in formal degree programs or as important dimensions of literature and history. In a special way, mysticism has attracted the attention of academicians, who have embarked on a fresh study of mysticism from historical, philosophical, and scientific viewpoints. In the midst of this awakened interest, the question naturally arises: What is the relation of mysticism to spirituality?

History of the Term "Mysticism"

Before we attempt to answer that question, it would be helpful to clarify the meaning of the term "mysticism" by taking a glance at its long history. The term is derived from a Greek root *mus*, contained in the verb *muein*, meaning to close the lips or eyes, and refers to the secrecy surrounding the mysteries or rites performed in ancient Greece, especially at Eleusis. In the Western Middle Ages the Latin term *mysticus* was often used to mean spiritual, with the connotation of something hidden or secret, especially in relation to the allegorical or symbolic interpretation of Scripture. Although *The Oxford English Dictionary* gives an example of the use of the term "mystic" in the fourteenth century, the following quotation from 1736 is the first example cited of the use of the term "mysticism": "How much nobler a Field of Exercise . . . are the seraphic Entertainments of Mysticism and Exstasy than the mean and ordinary Practice of a mere earthly and common Virtue!"[7] Note that the quotation associates mysticism with ecstasy, distinguishing it from the ordinary life of virtue. It is this meaning that dominates in modern usage. Mysticism suggests the higher forms of religious experience, with an emphasis on their intense, even ecstatic character and their proximity to union with God. Because of this, mysticism is distinguished from the general spiritual path and the ordinary life of virtue.

With this historical sketch as a backdrop, we can return to our question: What is the relation of mysticism to spirituality? Without attempting to formulate a technical definition, we can understand spirituality to refer to growth in the life of the Spirit, its conditions, its dynamics, and its finality. If we take the modern meaning of mysticism with its emphasis on higher states of consciousness, then mysticism would be a part of spirituality, but not coextensive with it. This leads us to distinguish between mystical spirituality and ordinary spirituality. What, then, is the relation between the two: between mysticism and the non-mystical journey? Is mysticism so far removed from the general spiritual journey that it has nothing to say to the majority of those on a spiritual quest? Do the mystics walk the cold heights alone leaving the rest of us in the valley or at the foot of the mountain? Can the mystic's intense— even ecstatic—experience reveal something about our own experience and our own spiritual journey? I believe that it can. The mystics themselves state and imply this, and a comparative study of mystical and non-mystical spirituality confirms it.

I believe, then, that the mystic's experience manifests in an intense often dramatic fashion the dynamics and structures of experience encountered by the majority of those on a spiritual journey. In a certain sense, the mystic is a pioneer or explorer who ventures into unchartered realms and returns to draw us a map and to plan an itinerary for our own journey. Although the mystic might have reached peaks we will only glimpse from afar and although he or she might have habitually taken a lofty trail, the overall terrain is similar and the paths often parallel. Granted our differences, we can profit greatly from the maps the mystics provide. If we learn how to follow their directions, we will discover that mystics are reliable and sure-footed guides for us as we proceed on our own spiritual journey.

In the course of this study, we will examine two maps sketched by classical mystical writers. First, we will explore the stages of purgation, illumination, and union in the spiritual journey, as illustrated in the mystical experiences of Augustine described in his *Confessions*. From this example, we will see how his mystical experiences revealed the nature of the soul as image of God, more precisely as image of the Trinity. This notion of the soul, as developed by Augustine in his book *On the Trinity*, forms the theological basis for the Christian spiritual journey and its various stages. This will lead us to our second map, sketched by Bonaventure in his treatise, *The Soul's Journey into God*, which describes the stages of the ascent whereby the soul as image of the Trinity proceeds through contemplation to union with God.

Augustine's Mystical Experience

Probably the most widely used map of the spiritual journey is that of purgation, illumination, and union. This pattern describes the three stages through which the person passes in the journey into God. When one begins the spiritual quest, perhaps in novitiate training, he or she tends to focus on the purgation of negative elements: sin, bad habits, evil tendencies, personality flaws that present obstacles to one's progress in the spiritual life. Later, after one matures, the focus of attention shifts from purgation to illumination, with the positive perception of spiritual values replacing the concentration on removing obstacles. This second stage is more contemplative, while the first was more ascetical. Finally, if the person continues to make progress and is given abundant graces by God, he or she may enter the final stage of union—of habitual intimacy with God as the climax of the spiritual journey in this life.

This is the more common understanding of the map of the journey, but there is an alternative. Instead of charting the prolonged periods in one's life, these stages reveal the dynamics of each significant movement forward. In this perspective, each moment in which we make progress involves an element of purgation, of illumination, and of union. This could happen in an instant or a very brief period, or in an event—such as the conversion of Augustine—which takes place over a longer period but is not extended over one's entire life. Rather it represents the dynamics of an organic process within days, weeks, or months in the drama of one's life.

In Augustine's conversion, illumination came first, leading to purgation, which in turn opened the way for a unitive experience. Having been buffeted by passions and lost in a maze of philosophical searching, Augustine came to a turning point in his life. He tells us that he read the books of the Platonists, where he found expressed the equivalent of the Christian doctrine of the Trinity; but he failed to find there the Incarnation. Through this reading, he tells us: "I was admonished to return to my own self, and, with you (God) to guide me, I entered into the innermost part of myself, and I was able to do this because you were my helper."[8] In this way Augustine begins his journey into the depths of his soul; and in so doing, he charts the inner way which countless Christian mystics would follow in the future. "I entered and I saw with my soul's eye (such as it was) an unchangeable light shining above this eye of my soul and above my mind." This light, he tells us, was not physical nor even like physical light. "It was higher than I, because it made me, and I was lower because I was made by it." He then identifies this light as God under the aspects of truth, eternity, and love: "He who knows truth knows that light, and he who knows that light knows eternity. Love knows it. O eternal truth and true love and beloved eternity! You are my God; to you I sigh by day and night."[9]

This encounter with God in the depths of his soul was an overwhelming experience for Augustine. It was primarily an experience of ultimate reality: "From afar you cried out to me 'I am that am.' And I heard, as one hears things in the heart, and there was no longer any reason for me to doubt. I would sooner doubt my own existence than the existence of that truth *which is clearly seen being understood by those things which are made.*"[10] In vivid terms, he describes his encountering God as the ultimate unchangeable reality: "In the flash of a trembling glance, my mind arrived at That Which Is."[11]

Purgation through Illumination

At the moment Augustine was illumined by the light of the divine unchangeable reality, that very light revealed to him his need for purgation. "You beat back the weakness of my sight, blazing upon me with your rays, and I trembled in love and in dread, and I found that I was far distant from you, in a region of total unlikeness."[12] The light continued to flood in upon his mind freeing him from the Manichaeism he had embraced for many years; for in experiencing God as the ultimate reality, he perceived how God and his creation were good, that there were not two first principles, one good and the other evil. In the divine light, he perceived how evil was not a positive substance but a lack of goodness, and therefore did not require a cause as such.

Then the light began to fade and he found himself slipping back into his old habits. "But I had not the power to keep my eye steadily fixed (on God); in my weakness I felt myself falling back and returning again to my habitual ways."[13] In discovering God in the depths of his soul, Augustine had undergone an intellectual conversion; his consciousness was permanently altered in such a way that he did not return to his old ways of perceiving reality. But his moral life was still disordered; his passions were still at war within him. He was in need of a comparable moral conversion. After his illumination, he needed a purgation that would bring his life into harmony with his newly acquired vision of reality. Not long after, this moral conversion followed, flowing out of the energy released by the illumination experience of his intellectual conversion.

In the next section of his *Confessions*, Augustine describes his moral conversion: "In my own temporal life everything was unsettled and *my heart had to be purged from the old leaven.*"[14] Through a painful process he eventually reached the climax of his moral conversion in a dramatic scene in a garden. He went apart alone, flung himself on the ground realizing that his former sins were holding him fast. In his misery, he cried out: "How long, how long this 'tomorrow and tomorrow'? Why not now? Why not finish this very hour with my uncleanness?" Then he heard a child's voice repeating in a singsong fashion: "Take and read, Take and read." He opened the Scriptures and read the passage from Paul: *Not in rioting and drunkenness, not in chambering and wantonness, not in strife and envying; but put ye on the Lord Jesus Christ, and make not provision for the flesh in concupiscence.* In reading that text, he felt his life put in order: "For immediately I had reached the end of this sentence it was as though my heart was filled with a light of confidence and all the shadows of my doubt were swept away." His conversion was so great that he found he had received not only the gift of chastity but that of celibacy: "For you converted me to you in such a way that I no longer sought a wife nor any other worldly hope."[15]

What is striking about Augustine's conversion is that purgation follows illumination and is derived from it. This is not the usual understanding of the relation of purgation to illumination in the first interpretation of the stages given above. When they are interpreted as reflecting three extended periods in a lifetime, purgation usually involves ascetical practices—especially in monasticism—of fasting, mortification, internal and external discipline in the overcoming of bad habits and the acquiring of virtues. Although many mystics practice penance and mortification—often to an extreme degree, as for example, in the life of Francis of Assisi—the mystics often achieve purgation through illumination. I believe that this dynamic functions also in psychoanalysis in its various forms in the twentieth century. As in the case of Augustine, psychoanalysis aims at a transformation of consciousness which in turn brings about an alteration of behavioral patterns. On a deeper spiritual level, a similar dynamic operates in the mystic's purgation through illumination.

Augustine's conversion was climaxed by a unitive experience which he shared with his mother shortly before her death. The two of them were together in Ostia, conversing about spiritual things. Augustine describes their experience as follows: "Then, with our affections burning still more strongly toward the Selfsame, we raised ourselves higher and step by step passed over all material things, even the heaven itself from which the sun and moon and stars shine down upon the earth." Above heaven they came to their own souls and went beyond their souls to God himself. "And as we talked, yearning towards this Wisdom, we did, with the whole strength of our hearts' impulse, just lightly come into touch with her, and we sighed and we left bound there the first fruits of the Spirit, and we returned to the sounds made by our mouths, where a word has a beginning and an ending."[16] With this, Augustine's conversion experience came to a completion. In this dramatic event of his life, the dynamics of illumination, purgation, and union completed their cycle, lifting him to a new level of spiritual existence where he would live out a life of rich interiority and boundless external productivity.

Soul as Image of God

In his mystical experience of illumination, Augustine discovered his soul as image of God. He found God present in the depths of his soul: as Eternity in his memory, as Truth in his intellect, and as Goodness in his will. This divine presence in the depths of the soul provides the ontological and theological basis for the spiritual life and for the spiritual journey. God was more intimate to Augustine than he was to himself; yet Augustine had not been aware of God's presence within himself. He had lived a life of superficiality, of illusion, of forgetfulness of his true self. This God image within him constituted his true self as distinguished from his more superficial or false self. This God image was the pearl of great price; once found it was to be cherished and cultivated. His conversion, then, was much more than a moral conversion; it was a discovery of the ontological basis of the spiritual life and of the direction of the spiritual journey. Augustine realized that he must grow as image of God: that he must remember, know, and love God in all phases of his life and in all the dimensions of creation. In his treatise *On the Trinity*, he analyzed in great detail the nature of the soul as image of God, and specifically as image of the Trinity. This study became the basis for the later mystical tradition's charting of the stages of spiritual growth, as for example, in Bonaventure's classic *The Soul's Journey into God.*

In 1259, Bonaventure, who had recently been elected the Minister General of the Franciscan Order, went to Mount La Verna, in Tuscany, to find peace and to search out his Franciscan roots. It was there, thirty-five years before, that Francis of Assisi had a mystical vision of a six-winged Seraph in the form of Christ crucified, after which he received the stigmata. While meditating on this mystical vision, Bonaventure perceived that it could symbolize the stages of the soul's journey into God. Since we are images of God, as Augustine discerned, and since creation bears the imprint of God as his vestige, we can contemplate the presence of God in all of creation and thus progress in our spiritual journey towards union with God. In this way Bonaventure sketched a map or itinerary which can guide us, through the various levels of reality to the goal of our spiritual quest. This map differs from the one we saw exemplified in Augustine's conversion. The latter charts the dynamic of internal transformation through purgation, illumination, and union; the former points out how we can proceed towards union with God through cultivating the illumination of contemplation.

Stages of Contemplation

Following Augustine's lead in the *Confessions*, Bonaventure takes us on a journey from the external world to the internal world of our consciousness to the higher realm of the divine. He bids us contemplate God in the outer world of matter, in the inner world of our faculties, and in God himself. This threefold division Bonaventure extends into six, with the six wings of the Seraph symbolizing the six stages of the soul's journey into God. In the first stage, we contemplate God in the material world. In the spirit of Francis of Assisi, he writes: "Let us place our first step in the ascent at the bottom, presenting to ourselves the whole material world as a mirror through which we may pass over to God, the supreme Craftsman."[17] In the second stage he bids us turn to our activity of sensation, analyzing our experience of beauty. From our pleasure and joy in beautiful things, he leads us to the beauty of the Trinity and to God's delight in the beauty of his inner Trinitarian life: "It is obvious that in God alone there is primordial and true delight and that in all of our delights we are led to seek this delight."[18]

In the third stage, Bonaventure guides us more deeply within ourselves, to the depths of our rational faculties of memory, understanding, and will. Here he bids us contemplate the image of God within us, deriving his understanding from Augustine, whose mystical experience, as we saw above, had illumined this reality. "See, therefore," he states, "how close the soul is to God, and how, in their operations, the memory leads to eternity, the understanding to truth, and the power of choice to the highest good."[19] In treating the fourth stage, he observes: "It seems amazing when it has been shown that God is so close to our souls that so few should be aware of the First Principle within themselves." Like Augustine he is aware that our attention is turned away from the God image, that we live in darkness and illusion, that we must be illumined by the rays of divine grace, and be awakened to our true selves. This transformation is the work of Christ, who leads us to grow in the spiritual life: "So our soul could not rise completely from the things of sense to see itself and the Eternal Truth in itself unless Truth, assuming human nature in Christ had become a ladder, restoring the first ladder that had been broken in Adam."[20]

In the fifth stage, we turn our gaze above, contemplating God as Being. "If God is called primary being," Bonaventure says, "eternal, utterly simple, most actual, and most perfect, it is impossible that he be thought not to be or to be other than unique. *Hear*, therefore, *Israel, your God is one God.* If you see this in the pure simplicity of your mind, you will somehow be bathed in the brilliance of eternal light."[21] Turning then to another perspective in the sixth stage, Bonaventure contemplates God as the self-diffusive Good. Since God is all-perfect, he must have the fullness of goodness. But since goodness must be self-diffusive, God must be self-diffusive in the highest degree. This brings Bonaventure into the mystery of the inner life of the Trinity, where the self-diffusion of the Good is completely actualized in the Trinitarian processions of the generation of the Son and the spiration of the Holy Spirit. The divine self-diffusive power is so great that not even creation can fully actualize it. "For diffusion in time in creation is no more than a center or point in relation to the immensity of the divine goodness."[22]

Having contemplated God in the material world, in the soul, and in God himself, we are now drawn by Bonaventure to the seventh and final stage of the spiritual-mystical journey. In this stage we leave behind all sense impressions, all intellectual activities, and pass over into the furnace of divine love. "In this passing over, if it is to be perfect, all intellectual activities must be left behind and the height of our affection must be totally transferred and transformed into God." In this stage, we should seek "darkness not clarity, not light but the fire that totally inflames and carries us into God by ecstatic unctions and burning affections. This fire is God, and *his furnace is in Jerusalem*; and Christ enkindles it in the heat of his burning passion."[23]

The Soul's Journey into God of Bonaventure is an excellent example of the thesis of this article. The work was inspired by the ecstatic mystical experience of Francis of Assisi at La Verna. The vision which Francis had in that experience of the six-winged Seraph in the form of Christ crucified becomes the symbol of the stages of the soul's journey into God. This journey culminates in the seventh stage, which is a state of mystical ecstasy in which one experiences divine love without sense impressions and without intellectual activity. Yet the intervening chapters, dealing with the six stages of the journey are not written on the ecstatic mystical level. Rather they are intended for all spiritual seekers, those committed to the spiritual quest, interested in prayer and contemplation, but who might not have received extraordinary graces. In these chapters Bonaventure begins with everyday experience and leads the reader into contemplative prayer in which he or she becomes aware of God's presence: first in the material world, then within the soul, and finally in the contemplation of God himself.

When Bonaventure contemplates God's presence within the soul, he follows the same path that Augustine charted in the mystical experiences we described earlier. However Bonaventure takes his point of departure from our ordinary experiences of memory, understanding, and love rather than from Augustine's dramatic, life-transforming experiences of God within his soul. Yet if one follows Bonaventure's everyday path, he or she could, with God's grace, be drawn to the same point as Augustine; for any of the six stages of contemplation can lead to mystical experiences if they are followed to their ultimate goal. Here, then, in *The Soul's Journey into God*, the itinerary of the spiritual journey encompasses mystical experience, not as something out of joint and unrelated to our spiritual growth, but as revealing the dynamics of the spiritual life. Whether they sketch the three stages of purgation, illumination and union, or the six stages of contemplation, the classic maps drawn by the mystics can be of assistance to all who have embarked on a spiritual journey.

Chapter 2:
Bernard of Clairvaux and
The Spiritual Path of Love:
A Global Phenomenon

In the history of Christian spirituality, Bernard of Clairvaux holds a distinguished place. He played a decisive role in the monastic reform of the twelfth century, stimulating the development of the newly founded Cistercian Order and infusing into its spirituality his own dynamic vision. He defended the autonomy of spirituality against what he thought was the destructive rationalism of Peter Abelard and the emerging Scholasticism, which in later centuries would drive a wedge between spiritual experience and rational consciousness. He gave impetus to two devotions that flourished in the later Middle Ages, becoming major forces in subsequent spirituality: devotion to Mary and to the humanity of Christ.

In a century that was unique in Western history for the cultivation of love, Bernard towered above his contemporaries. In his eulogies of human love, he echoed the troubadours, trouvères, and the writers of romance; but unlike his secular counterparts, he saw this love as a symbol of the soul's love for Christ, and he charted a journey through love to union with God. His achievement was so great that he has become the classic guide for those who follow the path of love in Christian spirituality. It is not fortuitous, then, that Dante chose Bernard as his spiritual guide at the climax of *The Divine Comedy*. After the love of Beatrice had drawn Dante to the highest heaven, Bernard took over the role of guide, leading him first to Mary and then to a vision of God that united him to "the Love that moves the sun and the other stars."[24]

The emergence of a spirituality of love, however, was not confined to Christianity in twelfth-century France. Quite the contrary! As has been observed by Richard Payne, the developer of the *Classics of Western Spirituality*, that was a great century for the spirituality of love in the world's religions.25 In various traditions and in diverse geographical areas, love was cultivated as a spiritual path with an intensity and a creativity that was unprecedented. In Judaism, for example, rabbis turned with new vigor to compose mystical commentaries on the *Song of Songs*. In the latter part of the twelfth century, the Kabbalah emerged in France and Spain. This complex mystical tradition provided a theoretical framework and practical techniques for activating the energy of love in the spiritual life. It highlighted the *Shekhinah*, or feminine aspect of God, and saw the integration of male and female energies as central to the spiritual life. This led, in the thirteenth century, to the composition of the *Zohar*, the classical Jewish mystical text expressing the love of God in the Middle Ages. In this context, the sexual union of husband and wife on the Sabbath gradually became a sacred ritual that participated in the union of the male and female aspects of God.

In Islam love also flourished—for example, in the writings of the Sufi masters 'Attâr, Ahmad al-Ghazâllî, and Ibn 'Arabî. They highlighted the theme that God is lovable in his divine beauty, which he has manifested through the beauty of creatures. With consummate literary skill, the Muslim authors turned to lyric poetry to express this spirituality of love, often addressing a beautiful woman as the manifestation of the divine Beloved. This tradition reached a peak in the thirteenth century mystical love poetry of Rumi.

In Hinduism the way of love or devotion (*bhakti*) attained a stage of development that established it as a major Hindu path throughout subsequent history. Inspired several centuries earlier by the Âlvâr and Nâyanâr love mystics of southern India, the path of love was given a philosophical-theological foundation in the twelfth century by Ramanuja. It was at this time that the love tradition spread to northern India, becoming a dominant force in Hindu spirituality. It was at this time, too, that the *Gîta Govinda* was composed, the Hindu counterpart to the *Song of Songs*, which celebrates erotic love as a symbol of the spiritual journey. Although of earlier origin, the Tantric traditions reached full development in this period, focusing on the feminine aspect of God, drawing on erotic experience, and incorporating ritual into the spirituality of love.

In Buddhism similar Tantric developments occurred in northern India, Nepal, and Tibet. In Japan in the twelfth century Honen established the school of Pure Land Buddhism. He and his disciple Shinran taught that it was not the strict discipline of Zen but the benevolent love or compassion of the Amida Buddha that leads to enlightenment. This tradition has become a major force in Japanese Buddhism.

In the context of world spirituality, then, Bernard of Clairvaux has played a special role. At a time when love was being cultivated in the world's religions in a new and creative way, it was Bernard who emerged in Christianity as the spiritual master of the path of love. Since, among the world's religions, Christianity gives preeminence to love, it required a master of exceptional talents to bring this central theme to a new level of self-consciousness and to chart a path that would lead Christians from the first stirrings of love to union with God. In the twelfth century Christianity was gifted with such a master in Bernard of Clairvaux.

Yet Bernard did not stand alone. In Christian Europe in the twelfth century, love was cultivated in both secular and religious circles. It flourished in the court and in the cloister. In southern France before the twelfth century, troubador poets had begun to awaken a romantic strain, singing the glories and the sorrows of the love between man and woman. In the twelfth century this love poetry flourished, and its themes were further developed in the genre of romance. Storytellers recounted the tragic love between Launcelot and Guinevere, between Tristan and Isolde. Through the romances of Chrétien de Troyes, written not far from Bernard's abbey, knights and ladies of the court were instructed in the gentle manners and sophisticated emotions that became part of the mystique of courtly love. This secular movement, which has contributed so much to the myth of romantic love in Western culture, did not produce an explicit spirituality of love. Yet it did contain the seeds of such a spirituality, which later blossomed in Dante.

In twelfth-century France, it was the cloister rather than the court that produced a spirituality of love. Were there influences between the two? Scholars still debate this point. Whatever the influences, mutual or not, this much is clear: As the century progressed, love became the central theme in the spiritual writers of the period. Like Bernard, many turned to producing commentaries on the *Song of Songs*, for example, William of St. Thierry and Richard of St. Victor. These two writers also composed theological treatises interpreting the Trinity in the light of human love. Aelred of Rievaulx composed a treatise entitled *On Spiritual Friendship*. Like the Platonists of Chartres, Hildegard of Bingen situated love in a cosmic setting. In this flourishing of the spirituality of love, Bernard played a leadership role, influencing this milieu by the power of his personality and position as well as by the depth of his spiritual wisdom.

As is characteristic of the twelfth century, Bernard bases his spirituality on experience. At the outset of his third sermon on the *Song of Songs*, he bids his monks examine their own experience. "Today," he says, "we read the book of experience." From the context, and throughout his writings, it is clear that he is concerned with religious experience, specifically the experience of affectivity, covering the entire spectrum from the initial awakening of love to mystical union with the Beloved. It would be wrong to see this as a mere evoking of emotion or sentimentality. Bernard and the major spiritual writers of the twelfth century drew from the deepest levels of affectivity—from those wellsprings of the spirit where affectivity and intellect are conjoined. Moreover, Bernard is acutely aware of the dynamics of love as a spiritual path. It is this path that he charts with intellectual brilliance. In his introduction to this volume, Jean Leclercq observes that Bernard's "unique and definitive distinction is due to his method of reconciling personal, subjective experience with universal, objective teaching." Far from ignoring or denigrating intellect, the twelfth-century spiritual writers achieved a new level of intellectual self-consciousness precisely in the realm of religious experience. For example, Bernard's contemporary Richard of St. Victor is credited with founding the discipline of speculative spirituality or speculative mysticism. The excitement that followed upon this new burst of intellect into the realm of spirituality led Richard to seek for "necessary reasons" for the Trinity—an outreach of intellect that the more hesitant Artistotelian theologians of the thirteenth century refused to pursue.

Not all of Bernard's spiritual writings deal directly with love, but in the total corpus of his works love is by far the dominant theme. Since he presents the climax of the spiritual journey as union with God in love, all of his writings can be seen as delineating stages in this process. Hence Evans has arranged the selections in this volume according to the order of the spiritual pilgrimages: "On Conversion," "On the Steps of Humility and Pride," "On Consideration," which deals with contemplation, "On Loving God," and "Sermons on the *Song of Songs*." The volume closes with a selection of letters, where the theme of love is also prominent.

It is in "Sermons on the *Song of Songs*" that Bernard's spirituality of love receives its most comprehensive expression. The central theme of these sermons is intimacy: the intimate love between the Bride and the Bridegroom, between the soul and Christ. The sermons begin with a longing for intimacy expressed in the first verse of the *Song of Songs*: "Let him kiss me with the kiss of his mouth." In Sermon 7, Bernard delivers a eulogy on the love between man and woman as the most intimate of human loves. Why does the *Song of Songs* use the image of bride and bridegroom? Because they are lovers and, as Bernard will explain, the most intimate of lovers. With great subtlety, he distinguishes the basic attitudes that constitute various relationships. Fear motivates a slave toward his master, desire for gain that of a worker toward his employer, knowledge that of a pupil toward his teacher, respect that of a son toward his father. But the one who asks for a kiss is a lover. "This affection of love," Bernard says, "excels among the gifts of nature, especially when it returns to its source, which is God." Because of the intimacy of their love, no names can be found that better express the love between the Word and the soul than those of Bridegroom and Bride. For they hold everything in common. "They share one inheritance, one table, one house, one bed, one flesh" (I.2).

Through the images of the bride and the bridegroom, Bernard describes at great length and with extraordinary sophistication the movement of the soul toward union with the Word. He does this with the full power of his passionate rhetoric as he orchestrates sensuous imagery to draw his hearers toward the heights of mystical affectivity. In the later sermons he describes, with remarkable delicacy and candor, his own intimate experiences of union with the Bridegroom.

In his symbolic interpretation of *The Song of Songs*, Bernard situates himself in an ancient tradition, which in its Christian strand goes back to Origen in the third century. In the prologue to his commentary on the *Song of Songs*, Origen states: "This book seems to me an epithalamium, that is, a wedding song, written by Solomon in the form of a play, which he recited in the character of a bride who was being married and burned with heavenly love for her bridegroom, who is the Word of God." Origen then proceeds to distinguish two allegorical meanings of the bride. "Whether she is the soul made after His image or the Church, she has fallen deeply in love with Him."[26] Although Bernard emphasizes the meaning of the bride as allegory of the individual soul, he also develops the second meaning, the bride as allegory of the Church.

In the patristic and medieval periods, allegory was looked upon not as a flight of fancy, but as a method of penetrating into a deeper level of the sacred text, based on the structure of reality and the very nature of the psyche. According to this perspective, God, in creating the universe, imprinted certain spiritual meanings into physical symbols, which could be discerned by a heightened spiritual sensibility nourished by Scripture and tradition. No wonder, then, that Bernard sees in the bride and bridegroom the most appropriate symbol for the soul aflame with love for the Word. The love between the bride and the bridegroom is a natural symbol—that is, structured into the very nature of reality—for the intimate love between the soul and God. As Bernard has eloquently expressed, no other human relation can achieve more intimate love than that of the bride and the bridegroom.

Moreover the two levels of the allegory—the soul and the Church—are not arbitrary. One can detect in this distinction the basis of a philosophy and theology of interpersonal and community relations. Of course, in this context the Church should be interpreted not as an institution, but as the community of believers. What is it, then, that makes such a community possible? The fact that the same Word is the Bridegroom of each individual soul. Thus the Word provides the basis of interpersonal and community relations since all are already related by being grounded in the same Word. It is this ground that is the ontological presupposition that makes interpersonal and community relations possible, and it is this ground that is awakened when these relations are activated.

These brief observations merely highlight some of the richness of Bernard's spirituality. The readers who explore this volume will be moved by the depth and sophistication of his teaching, as they will be carried along by his passionate eloquence, which shines through the translation. They will perceive those qualities that entitle him to a place of eminence not only in Christian spirituality in the twelfth century, but within the entire scope of its history and within the larger horizons of world spirituality.

Chapter 3
Franciscan Roots of Ignatian Meditation

To claim Franciscan roots for Ignatian meditation may seem surprising. The personalities of Francis of Assisi and Ignatius of Loyola stand at the opposite ends of a spectrum. Francis was a free spirit, a poet and singer of songs like the troubadors, a spontaneous leader who inspired thousands of followers but who left the organization and administration of his Order to others. In fact, in his spontaneity he produced a movement that seemed to defy institutionalization. Ignatius, on the other hand, was an able administrator, an organizer *par excellence*, a long-range strategist who could put his master plan into practice even in minute detail. His military experience shaped his natural gifts, which he placed at the service of spiritual goals. He had a genius for method, for orienting means to ends—for developing an institution, for spiritual discipline, and for meditation. The calculated methodology of Ignatius' *Spiritual Exercises* and the spontaneity of Francis' *Hymn of Brother Sun* mirror in literary form the differences in their lives and personalities.

The religious orders that these two saints founded reflect, at least in the popular mind, this same diversity. The Franciscans strive to imitate the simplicity of their founder, while the Jesuits have acquired a reputation for worldly sophistication, for crafty pragmatism, and for intellectual cultivation. The Franciscans place a primacy on poverty, the Jesuits on obedience. The Franciscans value love over intellect; the Jesuits esteem intellect highly, placing it at the service of the glory of God. Throughout the world the Jesuits are known for their intellectual achievement, for their colleges and universities, for their scholars who reach eminence not only in philosophy and theology but in secular fields as well. As we will see, this polarity is not completely accurate, since from the beginning the Franciscans developed a great intellectual tradition, which flourishes in this century in the high quality of their historical, critical research.

Granted the differences above, Franciscans and Jesuits share a common ground that provides the very foundation of their spiritualities. By reason of this common ground, Franciscans and Jesuits stand closer together than either group does to the Dominicans. This common ground is devotion to the humanity of Christ, which in each case flowered in meditation on the life of Christ. Both groups developed a Christocentric spirituality that looked back to the historical events of Christ's life as its point of departure. In this perspective, the Jesuits can be seen to be heirs of a tradition that was originally developed by the Franciscans in the thirteenth century, which was transmitted to subsequent centuries largely through Franciscan channels. Although Franciscan in origin and transmission, this tradition so permeated the religious sensibility of Western Christianity that it became a dominant feature of European culture as a whole.

In this essay, I will explore this common ground of devotion to the humanity of Christ. After a sketch of the historical background, I will show how this devotion emerged in Francis and the early Franciscan movement. Next I will show how it was developed into a method of meditating on the life of Christ by Bonaventure in his *Tree of Life*. Already in the thirteenth century this method contained all the basic elements of Ignatius' meditation on the life of Christ in the *Spiritual Exercises*, but without his self-conscious method. From Bonaventure's and Ignatius' texts I will draw out the essential element of this meditation, which I call the "mysticism of the historical event." By this I mean a distinct form of contemplative mystical consciousness whereby one attempts to enter into a significant event of the past in order to tap its spiritual energies. I claim that this is a specific form of mystical consciousness, meriting a place in any comprehensive typology of mysticism.

In the next section of the paper, I will examine how Bonaventure situated this "mysticism of the historical event" within the mainstream of Christian theology and spirituality. This can be illustrated by comparing his *Tree of Life* with his *Soul's Journey into God*. Finally, I will raise a question concerning Ignatius and his *Spiritual Exercises*: did Ignatius have a Bonaventure as Francis did? Francis did not integrate the devotion to the humanity of Christ, which he evoked, into the traditional theology of the Trinity, creation, the incarnation, and redemption. This task was performed by Bonaventure. Most importantly for our focus, Bonaventure integrated the mysticism of the historical event into the other modes of experiencing the mystery of Christ, chiefly through the fourfold interpretation of Scripture. Has there been, within the Jesuit tradition, an effort to link the Ignatian meditation on the life of Christ with other dimensions of the mystery of Christ and to situate the perspective of the *Spiritual Exercises* within a comprehensive theological and spiritual framework?

Although my title suggests an historical study, my approach will involve other elements. My concerns are historical but not exclusively so; they are historical, psychological, spiritual, and theological. I will begin with historical data, especially the analysis of texts from the past. Although I am concerned with the historical influence of the Franciscans on Ignatius, I am more concerned with the forms of consciousness they cultivated. In this sense, I have a psychological interest, which could best be described as typological phenomenology. By this I mean that through the method of phenomenological analysis I strive to clarify the distinct structure and dynamics of the type of consciousness expressed in a text. I am concerned with the psychological not for its own sake but for its relation to spirituality: how does this specific form of consciousness contribute to growth in the life of the Spirit? Finally, I ask how all of these elements can be encompassed within a theological vision that is rooted in the tradition and open to the future. Thus, in keeping with the mysticism of the historical event, I am studying history here as a resource for spirituality in the present and future.

Devotion to the Humanity of Christ

During the Middle Ages there occurred in western Europe a remarkable transformation of religious sensibility that affected the very core of Christian spirituality and decisively changed its direction for subsequent centuries. I am speaking of the emergence of devotion to the humanity of Christ, with its focus on the historical events of Christ's life, its desire to imagine and re-enact these events and to imitate Christ in the concrete details of his earthly life.[27] This transformation of sensibility was so deep and pervasive that it is difficult— even now, centuries later—to reconstruct what Christian spirituality was like before it occurred. The emergence of devotion to the humanity of Christ, then, is a watershed that divides Western Christianity from its Eastern counterpart, and Western Christianity itself into two millennia.

Although interest in the historical events of Christ's life is as ancient as the Synoptic Gospels, during its first thousand years Christian spirituality tended to focus on the Risen Lord rather than on the Jesus of history. Of course, this statement must be elaborated in any extensive historical survey; for my present purposes, however, I am merely painting a general picture, sketching the outlines of a trend, realizing full well that in a more detailed study I would have to take into account exceptions and make necessary qualifications. The focus on the Risen Christ was set by Paul himself, who did not know the historical Jesus and who protested against restricting the apostolic privilege to those who had known Christ in his earthly life: "Even if we did once know Christ, that is not how we know him now" (2 Corinthians 4:16).[28] For Paul, the Christian spiritual life does not focus on the Jesus of history but on the Risen Lord in the fullness of his Paschal Mystery, present to the faithful here and now.

In the Greek world, attention was directed to Christ as Logos—in his pre-existence in the Trinity, as the Pantocrator through whom creation was achieved, as the Bridegroom of the soul and of the Church, and as Risen Lord through whom the process of divinization is accomplished in the return of all things to the Father. This emphasis is seen especially in the Alexandrian school, in Clement and Origen, in Athanasius and the Cappodocians. Although the Antiocene school turned to the humanity of Jesus, its emphasis did not produce in the East anything comparable to the western medieval devotion to Christ's humanity. Among the Latin Fathers, the historical humanity of Christ did not play a central role. For example, Augustine discovered Christ through his presence as Logos in the soul. This led him to a painstaking analysis of the soul as image of the Trinity and not to a meditation on the historical events of Christ's life. In Benedictine monasticism and its derivatives, which dominated western spirituality in the early Middle Ages, once again the focus was on the Risen Lord rather than on the historical Jesus. The paschal mystery was celebrated each day in the conventional Mass and throughout the year in the liturgical cycle.

Another ingredient of monastic spirituality was the chanting of the divine office, which consisted chiefly of the Psalms. These were interpreted allegorically as referring to Christ, not primarily in concrete historical details to be imitated, but in foreshadowing the paschal mystery, in which the monks were participating in their own historical existence. Although the main focus of monastic spirituality was not on the historical Jesus, the roots of meditation on the life of Christ can be traced to the monastic *lectio divina*. This was a practice of private reading, chiefly of the Scriptures, which was carried out in a very slow and meditative fashion.[29] Although it was not restricted to the events described in the Gospel nor was it elaborated into a formal method, the monks did meditate at length on those passages which present the historical events of Christ's life.

The historical roots of meditation on the life of Christ, of course, go deeper than the practice of *lectio divina*. They are grounded in the fact that Jesus was an historical person, that the early Christians wrote accounts of the events of his life in their sacred books, and that they interpreted these events as having cosmic significance. They are also grounded in the characteristics of the Western psyche and in the development of European culture during the Middle Ages. True to its Roman origins, the Western psyche is primarily concerned with the concrete, the pragmatic, the moral, the legal, and the political. All of these concerns tie the Western psyche to the historical event. This Roman attitude can be seen in the Latin Fathers, whose writings by and large are less mystical and cosmic than those of the Greek Fathers. These fundamental Roman attitudes were retained as Europe was transformed by the barbarian invasions. They remained at the wellsprings of the Western psyche as it shaped its early medieval civilization.

In the burst of energy that has been called the renaissance of the twelfth century, certain factors intensified this Western interest in the concrete, the historical, and the human. The Provencal poets sang eloquently of human love; monks wrote penetratingly of human friendship. Travel increased, especially to shrines that housed the relics of saints—their bones, their garments, the objects they used in everyday life. Most of all, interest in the Holy Land reached a climax in the success of the First Crusade. Granted the complex economic, political, and social forces involved in the crusades, on the religious level they reflected and intensified the growing devotion to the humanity of Christ. The religious motive for the crusades was to free from Muslim control the places where Jesus was born, preached, and died, so that Christian pilgrims could walk the same streets that he did, touch the stones that he stood upon, kiss the tomb in which he was buried. The crusaders fought to capture and bring back to Europe the relics of Christ's human life: the true cross, the crown of thorns. Through the dramatic cultural event of the crusades, the imagination of western Europe was being intensely directed to the concrete, human, historical details of the life of Christ.

Francis to Ignatius

In the twelfth century, Bernard of Clairvaux, who was an agent in political events and preached a crusade, was the leading figure directly cultivating devotion to the humanity of Christ. It is true that his major work, *Sermons on the Song of Songs*, is in the classical tradition of the Risen Lord, drawing from the Origen tradition of allegorical interpretation of Christ as Logos, who is Bridegroom of the soul and the Church. Yet even in these sermons he develops the notion of the "carnal love of Christ." Notice, he says, "that the love of the heart is, in a certain sense carnal, because our hearts are attracted most toward the humanity of Christ and the things he did or commanded while in the flesh." Bernard advises that we should cultivate this love by imagining Christ in the events of his life: "The soul at prayer should have before it a sacred image of the God-man, in his birth or infancy or as he was teaching, or dying, or rising, or ascending." Bernard gives as the principal reason why God became man that "he wanted to recapture the affections of carnal men who were unable to love in any other way, by first drawing them to the salutary love of his own humanity, and then gradually to raise them to a spiritual love."[30] In his sermons on the feasts of the liturgical year, Bernard carries out his own advice on imaging the humanity of Christ. Each feast provides him with an event upon which he meditates in detail, evoking human emotions to draw us to imitation.

Against this background the leading actor in our drama appeared on the stage of the Middle Ages. He was Francis of Assisi, who more than any other saint or spiritual writer transformed religious sensibility in the direction of devotion to the humanity of Christ. Although his role in this process is widely acknowledged, it is not easy to analyze. Unlike Bernard, he did not propound a theory concerning the "carnal love of Christ;" nor do we have extant sermons like Bernard's, which develop a method of meditating on the historical events of Christ's life. Rather, Francis was first and foremost intent on imitating Christ in poverty and on creating a lifestyle based, as he believed, on the essence of the Gospel. He attempted to embody in his own person this lifestyle, even in concrete details. Finally, two years before his death, he received the stigmata, the marks of Christ's passion, in his feet, hands, and side. His followers interpreted this as the ultimate embodiment of his imitation of Christ and the ultimate seal of divine approval.

Bonaventure's biography describes how Francis came to the idea of his way of life: "One day when he was devoutly hearing a Mass of the Apostles, the Gospel was read in which Christ sends forth his disciples to preach and explains to them the way of life according to the Gospel: that they *should not keep gold or silver or money in their belts nor have a wallet for their journey, nor two tunics, nor shoes, nor staff"* (Matthew 10:9). When he grasped its meaning, he was filled with joy and said: "This is what I want; this is what I long for with all my heart." Bonaventure describes how Francis proceeded to carry out Christ's injunction quite literally: "He immediately took off his shoes from his feet, put aside his staff, cast away his wallet and money as if accursed, was content with one tunic and exchanged his leather belt for a piece of rope."[31] This insight was confirmed later when Francis and his first follower, Bernard of Quintavalle, went to the church of Saint Nicholas to seek God's direction. Francis opened the book of the Gospel three times—the first time to the words: "*If you will be perfect, go, sell what you have and give to the poor"* (Matthew 19:21); the second time to the words: "*Take nothing on your journey"* (Luke 9:3); and the third time to the words: "*If anyone wishes to come after me, let him deny himself and take up his cross and follow me"* (Matthew 16:24). "This is our life and our rule," Francis said, "and the life and rule of all who wish to join our company."[32]

In these Gospel texts, Francis perceived the poverty of Christ's lifestyle and that of his disciples during the years of his public ministry. It was the life of a wandering teacher and preacher who had no permanent home, who went about his ministry unencumbered by physical possessions. This image of the

Christ the "Poor Man" Francis strove to imitate with a certain radical literalness. In his approach, we see the essential elements of the emerging devotion to the humanity of Christ: a looking back to the Christ of history—here to his public ministry—a focusing on concrete details, and an imitation of Christ's virtue as embodied in these details. Although the central event here was Christ's public ministry, Francis drew attention also to the poverty of Christ's birth and death. Eventually, these two events became the central themes in the devotion to the humanity of Christ. This is not surprising, not only because of the drama of these events, but because it is precisely birth and death that establish the historicity of the human situation.

In 1223, Francis created a creche for the midnight Mass at Greccio. Although these cribs existed before this time, for example, in Santa Maria Maggiore in Rome, they did not play the role in Christian devotion that they have subsequently come to play as a result of Franciscan influence. According to Thomas of Celano in his *Vita Prima*, Francis contacted a friend, John of Greccio, and bade him prepare for the midnight Mass in the following way: "If you want us to celebrate the present feast of our Lord at Greccio, go with haste and diligently prepare what I tell you. For I wish to do something that will recall to memory the little Child who was born in Bethlehem and set before our bodily eyes in some way the inconveniences of his infant needs, how he lay in a manger, how, with an ox and an ass standing by, he lay upon the hay where he had been placed."[33] Celano proceeds to give a graphic account of the scene at the Mass. I will quote it at length since the passage indicates how Francis drew the people into the event by reproducing it dramatically:

> The manger was prepared, the hay had been brought, the ox and ass were led in. There simplicity was honored, poverty was exalted, humility was commended, and Greccio was made, as it were, a new Bethlehem. The night was lighted up like the day, and it delighted men and beasts. The people came and were filled with new joy over the new mystery. The woods rang with the voices of the crowd and the rocks made answer to their jubilation. The brothers sang, paying their debt of praise to the Lord, and the whole night resounded with their rejoicing. The saint of God stood before the manger, uttering sighs, overcome with love, and filled with a wonderful happiness. The solemnities of the Mass were celebrated over the manger and the priest experienced a new consolation.
>
> The saint of God was clothed with the vestments of the deacon, for he was a deacon, and he sang the holy Gospel in a sonorous voice. And his voice was a strong voice, a sweet voice, a clear voice, a

sonorous voice, inviting all to the highest rewards. Then he preached to the people standing about, and he spoke charming words concerning the nativity of the poor King and the little town of Bethlehem. Frequently too, when he wished to call Christ *Jesus*, he would call him simply the *Child of Bethlehem*, aglow with overflowing love for him; and speaking the word *Bethlehem*, his voice was more like the bleating of a sheep. His mouth was filled more with sweet affection than with words. Besides, when he spoke the name *Child of Bethlehem* or *Jesus*, his tongue licked his lips, as it were, relishing and savoring with pleased palate the sweetness of the words.[34]

With his charm, simplicity, and artistic creativity, Francis has made the birth of Christ come alive by transforming Greccio into Bethlehem. Through concrete detail and dramatic action, he has drawn the friars and lay people into becoming actors in the event. Through his choice of details he has highlighted the message of poverty implicit in the scene. It is not surprising, then, that some forty years later Bonaventure, at that time Minister General of the Franciscan Order, composed *The Tree of Life*, a series of meditations on the life of Christ, which sought to achieve with the imagination what Francis did with a dramatic stage-like setting. After recalling the Gospel account of the birth of Christ, Bonaventure focuses on the concrete details that convey the message of poverty and humility. Then he invites the reader to become an actor in the event, even more intimately than Francis did at Greccio. The following is the entire text of his meditation on the nativity:

Under the reign of Caesar Augustus, the *quiet silence* [Wisd. 18:14] of universal peace had brought such calm to an age which had previously been sorely distressed that through his decree a census of the whole world could be taken. Under the guidance of divine providence, it happened that Joseph, the Virgin's husband, took to the town of Bethlehem the young girl of royal descent who was pregnant. When nine months had passed since his conception, the King of Peace *like a bridegroom from his bridal chamber* [cf. 1 Par. 22:9; Ps. 18:6], came forth from the virginal womb. He was brought forth into the light without any corruption just as he was conceived without any stain of lust. Although he was great and rich, he became small and poor for us. He chose to be born away from a home in a stable, to be wrapped in swaddling clothes, to be nourished by virginal milk and to lie in a manger between an ox and an ass. Then "there shone upon us a day of new redemption, restoration of the past and eternal happiness. Then throughout the whole world the heavens became honey-sweet."[35]

> Now, then my soul,
> embrace that divine manger;
> press your lips upon and kiss the boy's feet.
>> Then in your mind
>> keep the shepherds' watch,
> marvel at the assembling host of angels,
> join in the heavenly melody,
> singing with your voice and heart:
>> *Glory to God in the highest*
>> *and on earth peace*
>> *to men of good will.*[36]

This tradition of meditation on the life of Christ flowed into the later Middle Ages chiefly through the *Meditationes vitae Christi*, at one time attributed to Bonaventure. Material from these meditations was incorporated into the *Life of Christ* of Ludolph of Saxony, which Ignatius of Loyola read while he was recuperating from the injury he sustained at Pamplona. It is interesting to compare Ignatius' meditation on the nativity in the *Spiritual Exercises* with Bonaventure's in *The Tree of Life*. Like Bonaventure, he recalls the history of the event in what he terms the first prelude: "The first prelude is to review the history of the Nativity. How our Lady, almost nine months with child, set out from Nazareth, seated on an ass, as may piously be believed, together with Joseph and a servant girl leading an ox. They are going to Bethlehem to pay the tribute that Caesar has imposed on the whole land." In the second prelude Ignatius becomes much more detailed and bids, "form a mental image of the scene and see in my imagination the road from Nazareth to Bethlehem. I will consider its length and breadth, and whether it is level or winding through valleys and over hills. I will also behold the place of the cave of the Nativity, whether it is large or small, whether high or low, and what it contains."[37] He continues with the points of the contemplation as follows:

> **The first point** is to see the persons: our Lady and St. Joseph, the servant girl, and the Child Jesus after his birth. I will become a poor, miserable, and unworthy slave looking upon them, contemplating them, and ministering to their needs, as though I were present there. I will then reflect within myself in order that I may derive some fruit.

The second point is to observe, consider, and contemplate what they are saying and to reflect within myself that I may derive some profit.

The third point is to observe and consider what they are doing: the journey and suffering which they undergo in order that our Lord might be born in extreme poverty, and after so many labors; after hunger and thirst, heat and cold, insults and injuries, He might die on the cross, and all this for me. I will then reflect in order to gain some spiritual profit.[38]

The Mysticism of the Historical Event

How should one assess this form of meditation? Is it a mere exercise of the imagination, to create an interesting, fanciful picture which stimulates a devotion that tends to be sentimental? Or is it rooted in deeper levels of the psyche and in the very structure of human existence? I believe that it is rooted in the very historicity of human existence and that it activates that level of the psyche whereby we draw out the spiritual energy from a past event. I have called this elsewhere "the mysticism of the historical event."[39] By that I mean that it constitutes a distinct category of mystical consciousness, comparable to nature mysticism or soul mysticism. It deserves to be called "mystical" since it differs from our everyday forms of waking consciousness, even those in which we simply recall an event from the past. Just as in nature mysticism we feel united to the material world, so in this form of mysticism we feel part of the historical event—as if we were there, as eye-witnesses, participating in the action, absorbing its energy.

The mysticism of the historical event has both a secular form and a religious form. For example, if we visit the site of a famous battle, Marathon or Waterloo perhaps, we might feel gripped by the power of the place as the spot where a great event occurred. In our imagination we might glimpse scenes from the battle and feel present to the event as if we were actually immersed in its action, drawing on its energies as a decisive event in our own cultural history. We may experience this exclusively on the secular level; or, in the case of the life of Christ, we move through the event into various levels of religious meaning.

During the Middle Ages, the mysticism of the historical event was directed chiefly to the moral meaning of the event, as can be seen in the attitude of Francis, Bonaventure, and Ignatius toward the nativity scene. The setting, with the ox and the ass, revealed the humility and poverty that Christ was presenting to us for imitation. In terms of the fourfold sense of Scripture, which was widely explored in the Middle Ages, the mysticism of the historical event focused on the literal sense by recalling the narrative, then moved to the moral sense by drawing out an example of a virtue to be imitated. This would lead to the two deeper senses: the allegorical and the anagogic. Technically, the allegorical sense deals with the way an event in the Old Testament foreshadows Christ and his work of redemption. This refers to the fullness of the paschal mystery, involving the incarnation, death, and resurrection of Christ as effecting a cosmic transformation. Finally, the anagogic sense refers to the union of the soul with God in mystical union in this life or in eschatological fulfillment in eternity.

Since events in the life of Christ have meaning on all these levels, they should draw us beyond the mere moral level into the allegorical and anagogical. In this way, the mysticism of the historical event reaches its fullness, for it becomes a gateway into other modes of mystical consciousness. It is freed from the problems of superficiality and sentimentality that are inherent in it. Because it deals with human emotions—tenderness for the infant at Bethlehem or compassion for the suffering Saviour on the cross—it might remain merely emotional and not open up to the deeper religious affectivity on the allegorical and anagogical levels.

In order to bring the mysticism of the historical event to its fullness, there is need to situate it within the various levels of mystical consciousness and within a theological vision that can clarify and sustain these forms of consciousness in an organic synthesis. In the case of Francis, Bonaventure provided such a spiritual and theological context. His *Soul's Journey into God* can be seen as a companion piece to *The Tree of Life*, for it presents various forms of mystical or contemplative consciousness in the pattern of an ascent or journey towards union with God. In his prologue, Bonaventure tells us that he took his inspiration from the vision that Francis had on Mount La Verna in 1224, when he received the stigmata: the vision of a six-winged Seraph in the form of the Crucified. He says: "The six wings of the Seraph, therefore, symbolize the six steps of illumination that begin with creatures and lead up to God, whom no one rightly enters except through the Crucified."[40] In each of the succeeding chapters, he explores one of these forms of contemplation. He contemplates God's presence first in the material universe, then in our act of sensation, in the faculties of the soul, in these same faculties reformed by grace, in God as Being, and in God as the Good. Although there are six stages, they form a pattern of three major types: nature mysticism, soul mysticism, and God mysticism. In each of these, there is a distinct way of experiencing the mystery of Christ. In nature mysticism, he is experienced as the cosmic Christ, through whom the universe has been created. All creatures—

from the earthworm to the sun—reflect the eternal Word as their Exemplar. In soul mysticism, Christ is the Bridegroom of the soul, more intimate to me than I am to myself. In God mysticism, he is the eternal Word, the Image of the Father who is generated from the Father's fountain-fullness. Throughout the soul's journey, Christ is the vehicle of passage into the various forms of mystical consciousness, both as the God-man and as the crucified Redeemer. The crucified Christ is for Bonaventure the vehicle of the passage into mystical union because he is the vehicle of cosmic transformation in his incarnation death, and resurrection. It is into this larger framework of contemplation that the mysticism of the historical event in *The Tree of Life* should be placed. In this way the humanity of Christ is not limited to its historicity but opens up to the fullness of the mystery of Christ. It is here that the types of contemplation correspond to the fourfold sense of Scripture: *The Tree of Life* explores the literal and moral senses; the *Soul's Journey Into God* explores the allegorical and anagogic.

The *Soul's Journey Into God* contains a comprehensive theological vision, which Bonaventure developed extensively in his other works. This vision is founded on a dynamic Trinitarian theology in which the Father is seen as the fountain-fullness of the divinity, who expresses himself in his perfect Image and Word. Bonaventure sees this eternal self-diffusion as realization of the fullness of the principle that the Good must be self-diffusive.[41] In generating the Son, the Father produces in the Son the archetypes of all he can make *ad extra*, so that when he freely creates, the realm of creatures reflects the divine Word and is oriented to the Word as its final goal. This exemplaristic metaphysics is the way in which Bonaventure provides a theoretical structure for Francis' seeing God's reflection in all creatures. Because the Son is the Exemplar of the cosmos and the light of Truth shining in the soul, he becomes incarnate in order to illumine human beings and lead them back to the Father. In his final theological synthesis, the *Collations on the Hexaemeron*, Bonaventure presented a theological vision with Christ as the center. In his eternal generation he is the center of the Trinity; in his incarnation he is the center of the cosmos; in his death and resurrection he is the center of the process of cosmic transformation; and in his ascension and return to the Father he is the center drawing all things to their fulfillment. This rich theological vision is the appropriate setting for the mysticism of the historical event that Bonaventure developed in *The Tree of Life*.

Conclusion

This study suggests further questions concerning the *Spiritual Exercises* in the light of the history of devotion to the humanity of Christ and the Franciscan phase of this development. Francis, who gave a dramatic impetus to this devotion, had Bonaventure to develop his imitation of Christ into a form of meditation remarkably similar to the Ignatian method. But Bonaventure did much more. He integrated the mysticism of the historical event into the spirituality of the previous millennium—the spirituality of the Risen Christ, the Pantocrator, the Bridegroom of the soul; and he situated this multi-dimensional spirituality within a highly developed theological vision, based on the doctrine of the Trinity and Christocentricity. Did Ignatius have a Bonaventure? In his era and the subsequent history, how was his mysticism of the historical event subsumed into the larger spiritual tradition and into comprehensive theological visions? Is there reason to think that Bonaventure himself could play that role also for Ignatius? For example, his *Soul's Journey Into God* could well be used to supplement Ignatius' "Contemplation to Attain Divine Love." Its theological vision could provide a compatible context for the Christocentricity of the *Spiritual Exercises.*

In the twentieth century, it may well be that Karl Rahner has played Bonaventure's role. His own theological vision, which is very similar to Bonaventure's, provides an appropriate framework for the spirituality of the *Spiritual Exercises.*

Whether the theologian be Bonaventure or Rahner, the focus on the historical Jesus of both Francis and Ignatius calls for a guide to lead one according to the principle that Bernard of Clairvaux articulated at the very emergence of this devotion: the carnal love for Christ should lead us into spiritual love—ultimately into the fullness of the mystery of Christ.

Chapter 4
The Mysticism of the Historical Event

The devotion to the humanity of Christ issues in a form of mysticism which I will call "the mysticism of the historical event." In this type of consciousness, one recalls a significant event in the past, enters into its drama and draws from it spiritual energy, eventually moving beyond the event towards union with God. Of course, for Christians the significant events were those of the life of the historical Jesus, especially his birth at Bethlehem and his death and resurrection at Jerusalem. Although this type of consciousness was present in Christianity from the beginning, especially in the liturgy, it emerged in the thirteenth century in a new form and with new vigor. Under the impetus of Francis, it developed a specific form of meditation which became the characteristic form of Christian meditative prayer for centuries. In this form of prayer, one imagines the physical setting of the event—the place, the persons, the circumstances, for example the birth of Jesus in the stable at Bethlehem, with Mary and Joseph, an ox and an ass. However one does not remain a detached spectator, but enters into the event as an actor in the drama, singing with the angels and worshipping the infant with the shepherds. This immersion in the event opens its spiritual meaning—for example its message of poverty and humility—draws us into its deeper archetypal significance and leads ultimately to union with God. Cultivated in the Franciscan milieu, this form of prayer reached its culmination in *The Spiritual Exercises* of Ignatius of Loyola, where it was developed into one of the most systematic techniques of prayer in the history of Christian spirituality.

It is important to recognize "the mysticism of the historical event" as a distinctive form of mystical consciousness. Without it a typology of Christian mysticism would be incomplete, and yet it has not been adequately isolated or identified. If this is lacking in one's typology, it would be impossible to study accurately the history of Christian mysticism from the thirteenth century to the present, especially its development from Francis to Ignatius of Loyola. Furthermore, its inclusion in one's typology throws light upon the wide variety and inner tensions in the forms of Christian mysticism—from the ahistorical, world-transcending forms of speculative Neoplatonic mysticism to the focus on the concrete, human, dimensions of the mysticism of the historical event. Once these poles are isolated and identified, then it is possible to study the attempts and techniques employed throughout history to integrate them, whether successfully or not.

In proposing this category, I must clarify what I mean by "the mysticism of the historical event." In a generic sense, it belongs to that form of consciousness whereby we remember a past event, of our own lives or of our collective history. But it is more than merely recalling, for it makes us present to the event and the event present to us. This consciousness has a secular and a religious form. For example, when we visit a place where a great event occurred, especially a battlefield like Waterloo or Gettysburg, we can feel the power of the event—as a moment when thousands clashed and died and where the flow of history itself was altered. This experience of presence may be so strong that we feel ourselves swept up into the action of the event as if we ourselves were fighting in the battle. In and through our immersion in the event, we can discern its meaning as it reveals mankind's struggle for justice and power. If the event is religious, then its revelatory power is greater; for it manifests God's plan of salvation history and through salvation history God himself. For this reason medieval Christians flocked to shrines, where saints were martyred or buried. They especially wished to make a pilgrimage to the Holy Land, to walk the streets that Jesus walked and to visit the site of his birth, his crucifixion, and resurrection. If they could not make the physical journey, they could at least imagine they were in the Holy Land, present to the great religious events that happened there.

Some might argue whether this type of consciousness should be called mystical. I believe it is legitimate to designate it as such for two reasons. First, it is different from our everyday forms of consciousness, even different from our ordinary modes of recalling the past. In it we transcend the present moment and are transported into the past, entering into a unity with a past event that manifests its meaning. Such consciousness is analogous to nature mysticism, where we have a similar experience with regard to space. There is another reason to consider it mystical, because in its religious form it provides a path to another form of transcendence, namely, contact with God. The great religious events are seen as modes of God's manifestation to us and of our union with God. Again this is analogous to nature mysticism. In its religious form, our union with nature becomes a mode of God's communication of himself to us through his creation and of our union with him by perceiving his presence in the physical world.

If Francis was innovative in evoking the mysticism of the historical event," it should not be surprising that he is equally innovative in nature mysticism. Considered the prime example of a nature mystic in the history of Christianity, he took spontaneous joy in the material world, singing its praises like a troubadour poet in his "Canticle of Brother Sun." With a disarming sense of immediacy, he felt himself part of the family of creation, rejoicing in the least significant creature—in an earthworm or a cricket—and seeing God's reflection everywhere. As is the case with the mysticism of the historical event, this is a far cry from Neoplatonic speculative mysticism, which focuses on an abstract cosmological structure and which turns quickly from the material world and its individual creatures to scale the metaphysical ladder to the spiritual and divine realms by means of universal concepts.

If we were to search for a position within the Middle Ages itself to view Francis as innovator, we could find no better ground than Bonaventure's mystical writings. Minister General of the Franciscan Order at a crucial point in its history, he gained the title of its Second Founder. Along with Thomas Aquinas, he is considered one of the two major philosopher-theologians of the thirteenth century. His mystical treatises are among the classics of the genre. Writing several decades after Francis's death, Bonaventure attempted a double task: (1) to situate Francis' experience within the mainstream speculative, metaphysical, cosmological Neoplatonic tradition; and (2) at the same time to extend this tradition to encompass the devotional, Christ-centered focus of Francis, with its mysticism of the historical event. In his masterpiece, *The Soul's Journey into God*, he has written the *summa* of medieval Christian mysticism, for he attempts to give a typology of the major strands of medieval mystical consciousness that preceded Francis and at the same time to integrate the new Franciscan sensibility into this framework. His achievement here is not unlike that of Thomas Aquinas in theology. What Thomas achieved for Aristotle in theology, Bonaventure did for Francis in mysticism.

The remainder of our investigation will be a case study of transition in medieval mysticism. We shall begin with an exploration of Francis's mystical experience, drawn from historical documents and analyzed phenomenologically. We shall then see how Bonaventure integrated Francis's experience into the mainstream, speculative, Neoplatonic tradition in his treatise *The Soul's Journey into God*. Already in this work the image of Christ is central, though not explored in detail or treated devotionally. Bonaventure's later work, *The Tree of Life*, comprises a classical expression of the mysticism of the historical event in the form of an extended meditation on events in the life of Jesus. His treatment of Christ the Centre in his *Collations on the Hexaemeron* constitutes the final stage of his integrative process: it deals with Christ speculatively, situating him within the Neoplatonic metaphysical and cosmological scheme. In this way Bonaventure draws the innovations of Francis' experience into the established tradition, and at the same time transforms the tradition by these very innovations.

Chapter 5
The Coincidentia Oppositorum in the Theology of Bonaventure

In his extensive study of comparative religion, Mircea Eliade has analyzed the most fundamental religious pattern as that of hierophany, or the manifestation of the sacred. He has further analyzed hierophany as involving a coming together of opposites: of the sacred and the profane, the infinite and the finite, the eternal and the temporal. This union of opposites has been expressed throughout the history of religions by various forms of the ancient symbol of the *coincidentia oppositorum*. In *Patterns in Comparative Religion*, Eliade writes:

> This coming-together of sacred and profane reality produces a kind of breakthrough of the various levels of existence. It is implied in every hierophany whatever, for every hierophany shows, makes manifest, the coexistence of contradictory essences: sacred and profane, spirit and matter, eternal and non-eternal, and so on. That the dialectic of hierophanies, of the manifestation of the sacred in material things, should be an object for even such complex theology as that of the Middle Ages serves to prove that it remains the cardinal problem of any religion. One might even say that all hierophanies are simply prefigurations of the miracle of the Incarnation, that every hierophany is an abortive attempt to reveal the coming together of God and man.[42]

Eliade's reference to the theme of hierophany in medieval theology calls to mind Bonaventure, whose thought is primarily focused on the reflection of God in all levels of the universe and who sees the theophanic cosmos reaching its fullness in the hierophany of Christ. If, as Eliade says, hierophany is the basic religious problem, it would seem that Bonaventure's vision penetrates to the very essence of the religious sphere. And if medieval theology has brought this essential element to a high level of self-consciousness and has given it a rich expression, we can say that within medieval theology Bonaventure provides one of the most self-reflective and multi-dimensional expressions of the theophanic tradition.

Eliade's study throws light on the depth and richness of Bonaventure's thought, as seen against the background of the history of theology and comparative religion. At the same time, Eliade provides a point of view from which to study Bonaventure. If theophany is the central pattern of religion and if Bonaventure's thought is primarily concerned with this issue, it would be of paramount importance that our frame of reference for studying his thought should be such that it is coherent with the structure of theophany. Our framework must neither falsify nor distort Bonaventure's theophanic vision; rather it should clarify its dimensions. That is to say that our theoretical model for gaining a self-reflective awareness of Bonaventure's thought should be compatible with the metaphysical structure of his thought.[43] We must select the proper theoretical model for studying the metaphysics of theophany. Eliade indicates that the proper model is that of the *coincidentia oppositorum*, for in theophany the opposites come together: the absolute and the relative, the infinite and the finite, the eternal and the temporal.

In our present study we will attempt to analyze Bonaventure's theology by using the theoretical model of the *coincidentia oppositorum*. We are not attempting to make a judgment on the validity of Bonaventure's metaphysics of theophany; nor are we attempting to justify the logical model of *coincidentia oppositorum*. Rather we are taking as a working hypothesis that the *coincidentia oppositorum* is the proper model for studying Bonaventure's thought. Then by analyzing his thought in relation to this model, we hope to verify our hypothesis, and at the same time, through the model throw light upon the depth and significance of his metaphysics of theophany as well as its high degree of self-consciousness and inner coherence.

It is of paramount importance that one have the proper theoretical model in studying theophany. For example, there are two theoretical models that would cloud or distort the study. First, one might use the model of the participation of created forms in the class structure of genus and species. Although theophany is found on all levels of classes, as is clear from Bonaventure's doctrine of vestige, theophany itself cannot be analyzed by using a class model. For God is above classes and categories. If one were to stay within the limited structures of the class world, he would never encounter theophany. Secondly, one might use an atomistic model, in which opposites remain forever separated and even repel each other. In this case one would reason that God is infinite and man finite; since there is an infinite abyss between them, theophany is logically impossible. Such a model merely assumes that there is no coincidence of opposites. It is true that in a universe in which there is no coincidence of opposites, theophany is impossible. However, it is not necessary to posit such a universe since one can conceive a theoretical model of a universe in which the opposites actually coincide. In such a universe theophany would not only be possible, but would be the law of the deepest metaphysical reality.

Thus we can see the problems of using an improper model. If one would merely assume that Bonaventure is using the class model or the atomistic model, or if one were to criticize Bonaventure's thought by taking one of these two models as a norm, then he would fail to touch the basic philosophical and religious experience out of which Bonaventure's thought grows. He would also be inclined to judge Bonaventure's vision as lacking logical coherence and ontological foundations. We believe that some of the misunderstanding and criticism of such Bonaventurian doctrines as illumination, exemplarism and the centrality of Christ has been due to viewing his thought through an improper model. Hence, in analyzing Bonaventure's thought through the model of *coincidentia oppositorum*, we hope to throw light not only on theophany as a whole, but on specific areas of his thought where theophany is central: e.g., the epistemology of illumination, the metaphysics of exemplarism, the centrality of Christ in the cosmos and the dynamic expressionism at the core of Trinitarian life.

When we speak of the *coincidentia oppositorum* in Bonaventure, we do not mean that he used the term to characterize his thought or that he drew this model into complete self-reflection and charted its structure and logic as Nicholas of Cusa did at a later date.[44] We mean that the *coincidentia oppositorum* is implicit in his thought, but implicit in such a way that it provides the basic pattern of his metaphysics, his logic and his rhetoric. His use of its dynamics is so consistent and firm, that it indicates he was aware of it as a method and used it consciously as such, although he did not bring it into self-reflection as a logical model.

Since we believe that the *coincidentia oppositorum* is a key to understanding the whole of Bonaventure's thought, it would be possible to explore his use of the model by studying in turn the major themes of his thought. But we have another possibility. Because the *coincidentia oppositorum* is a factor in his rhetoric, he has the tendency to express in a compact way the whole of his thought in a single work, such as the *Itinerarium*, or even in a short passage within a work. Thus a brief passage becomes a microcosm in which the reader can view the macrocosm of Bonaventure's entire thought. Since this is the case, we can choose such a text, which can serve as a *minimum* to coincide with the *maximum* of his thought as a whole. We have chosen the first of the *Collationes in Hexaemeron*.[45] We have made this choice for two reasons: first, the *collatio* presents in an analytic way a complete cosmic vision beginning with the generation of the Son from the Father, proceeding through creation, the Incarnation and redemption, and leading back to God as final end. In each of the major sections Bonaventure analyzes the theophanic structure of the cosmic process by means of the *coincidentia oppositorum*. Secondly, the entire *collatio* is focused on Christ as the *medium* or center, in whom all the opposites coincide, and through whom they reach their dynamic completion. For Bonaventure, as for Eliade, the Incarnation is looked upon as the great hierophany, in which all other hierophanies have their ultimate meaning and to which they all point.

Before beginning our analysis of the first *Collatio in Hexaemeron*, it would be wise to make some observations on Bonaventure's use of the *coincidentia oppositorum* in the *Itinerarium*.[46] A detailed analysis of Chapters 5-7 reveals that their metaphysical, logical, and rhetorical structure is that of the coincidence of opposites. This is certainly one of the clearest and most striking examples of the pattern in Bonaventure's works. In Chapter 5, Bonaventure turns his gaze to contemplate God in his unity through his name which is Being. He bids the reader gaze in admiration on the divine being, which is the first and the last, eternal and yet the most present, most simple and the greatest, most actual and most changeless, most perfect and without measure, supremely one and yet possessing all aspects of the multiplicity.[47] Having been amazed at the coincidence of opposites in the divine essence, the reader turns his gaze to the Trinity and is overcome with wonder. For there he sees a remarkable coincidence of dynamic self-expression and intimate interpenetration: of supreme communicability with individuality of persons, supreme consubstantiality with plurality of hypostases, supreme similarity with distinct personality, supreme equality with ordered procession, supreme coeternity with emanation, supreme mutual intimacy with a sending forth.[48]

If we wondered at the coincidence of opposites in the divine nature and the Trinity, we will be struck with wonder when we turn our gaze to Christ and see in him the first principle joined with the last, God joined with man, the eternal joined with time-bound man, the most simple with the most composite, the most actual with the one who suffered and died, the most perfect and boundless one with the insignificant. If we wondered at the coincidence of plurality and unity in the Trinity, look at Christ in whom a personal unity exists with a trinity of substances and a duality of natures.[49] When we gaze at Christ, in whom are joined the first and the last, the highest and the lowest, the circumference and the center, the Alpha and the Omega, the caused and the cause, the Creator and the creature,[50] we will be overcome with admiration and pass over to the stage of mystical contemplation which Bonaventure describes in his seventh chapter. Hence, the meditation on Christ as the *coincidentia oppositorum* is precisely the way to mystical elevation, because Christ is the way and the door, the ladder and the vehicle.[51]

This treatment of the coincidence of opposites in the *Itinerarium* can serve as a backdrop for our study of the first *Collatio in Hexaemeron*. In the *Itinerarium*, the coincidence of opposites emerges in the fifth and sixth levels of contemplation and is seen primarily is the divine nature and the Trinity; finally Christ is seen as the extraordinary coincidence of opposites. The first *Collatio in Hexaemeron* is much more Christological in focus and cosmic in sweep. Christ is seen as the *medium*, uniting in himself all the opposites, both in the Trinity and in the cosmos. Hence Bonaventure sees Christ as a sevenfold *medium: medium metaphysicum, physicum, mathematicum, logicum, ethicum, politicum, theologicum*.[52] Bonaventure first considers Christ as the *medium metaphysicum* and grounds his consideration in the generation of the Son from the father. As *medium metaphysicum* the Word embodies three types of the coincidence of opposites: The first is concerned with the Trinity itself; the second with the Trinitarian basis of creation; and the third with knowledge.

First: within the Trinity itself, Bonaventure considers the Son as the *persona media Trinitatis*:

> *Istud est medium personarum necessario: quia, si persona est, quae producit et non producitur, et persona, quae producitur et non poducit, nesessario est media, quae producitur et producit*.[53]

This analysis views the Son as performing a mediating function within the Trinitarian life, linking the productive and receptive aspects of the deity. For the Father is the generating source, the *fontalis plenitudo*, the *principium originans*. At the opposite pole, the Holy Spirit is the person who is produced and does not produce, and hence can be called *spiratio passiva*. As Bonaventure observes, between these poles, there must be a *persona media*, who contains the opposites within himself and thus holds the poles in union. This *medium* is the Word, who is produced and produces. This type of coincidence is that of complementary opposites; the productive and receptive are complementary aspects of the divinity. Of course, the receptive does not imply limit or potency, but here refers to a pure perfection which is had in its absolute form in the divinity. In God are reconciled the opposites of absolute productivity and absolute receptivity. They are reconciled, but not merged. This is accomplished by the *persona media*, who acts as the unifying force of the opposites and the intensification of their differences. Hence one opposite does not resist the other, or absorb the other, or subordinate the other. They are held in absolute and eternal tension—eternally secure in their autonomy, yet nourished by their very differences. Thus by the union of opposites in the *persona media*, absolute unity and difference are achieved in the totality.

The view of the Word as *persona media*, uniting the polar aspects of the Father and the Spirit may seem static. The coincidence of complementary opposites, like the coincidence of the *maximum* and the *minimum*, seems to have a static aspect. Yet Bonaventure's thought is alive with dynamism. His most profound view of the Trinity is that of the dynamic good which is infinitely self-diffusive. This diffusion takes place by the divine expressionism, in which the Father expresses himself in his perfect image of the Son, who becomes the *medium* for the emanation of the Spirit, who completes the Trinity.[54] Thus the Word is the *medium*, not only the midpoint, but the dynamic means through which the Father objectifies himself and through which he returns to himself in the union of the Spirit. Thus there is within the Trinity a dynamism of emanation and return, which is mediated in the Son, who is the ground of both. This emanation and return in the Trinity becomes the archetypal ground for all emanation and return in the case of the created world. Thus within the Trinitarian life, the opposites of emanation and return are reconciled dynamically in the word.

The Trinitarian life is viewed by Bonaventure as the ground for the second level of the coincidence of opposites. This level is concerned with the coincidence of God and creation: the infinite and the finite, the absolute and the relative, the unchanging and the changing, the eternal and the temporal, the one and the many. How are these opposites joined? Once again it is by the Word as the *medium metaphysicum*. Just as he is the *medium* uniting the opposites in the Trinity, so he is the *medium* uniting the opposites of the Creator and the creature. It is precisely in his eternal generation from the Father, that the Son reconciles the opposites of the infinite and the finite. For in generating the Son, the Father produces in the Son all that he can create:

> *Pater enim ab aeterno genuit Filium similem sibi et dixit se et similitudinem suam similem sibi et cum hoc totum posse suum; dixit quae posset facere, et maxime quae voluit facere, et omnia in eo expressit, scilicet in Filio seu in isto medio tanquam in sua arte.*[55]

Bonaventure sums up his position in the compact statement: "*Verbum ergo exprimit Patrem et res, quae per ipsum factae sunt.*"[56] Therefore the Word expresses the Father and the things that were made through him [the Word]. As the eternal generation is the basis of expressionism in the Trinity, so it is the basis of exemplarism in creation. The eternal generation provides the theological foundation and philosophical articulation for Bonaventure's vision of the theophanic universe. His most basic religious experience is that of theophany. He is aware of the presence of God in all things, and he contemplates the reflection of God throughout the universe. This religious experience of theophany, or hierophany, is, as Eliade has indicated, precisely an awareness of the coincidence of opposites: the sacred and the profane, the eternal and the temporal. Bonaventure's analysis of the metaphysical roots of hierophany leads him to the Word, in whom the opposites coincide. For all temporal things have an eternal existence in the eternal Word. In him the temporal and eternal are united; in him the opposites coincide. Hence both the religious experience of hierophany and its philosophical articulation reveal the logic of the coincidence of opposites.

As was the case in the Trinity, the coincidence of opposites does not produce a static balancing of the scales of being. Rather it inaugurates a dynamic process. In the eternal generation, in which the *rationes aeternae* are produced in the Word, the absolute and the relative coincide from the side of the absolute. However, in temporal creation, where the *rationes aeternae* are embodied in space and time, the relative and absolute coincide from the side of the relative. But the form created in time is so embedded in its *ratio aeterna* that it is swept up in a dynamic return to its source. Hence the entire universe is *en route*; the cosmos is pursuing an *itinerarium in Deum*. Since the Word is the *medium* uniting the eternal and the temporal, he embodies within himself another coincidence of opposites; namely, the beginning and the end, the Alpha and the Omega. All things emanate from him; and since he is the eternal exemplar of the temporal, all things return through him to the unity of the Father; for, as Bonaventure says, *"Verbum... principaliter ducit nos ad Patris congregantis unitatem."*[57] The Word... leads us to the unity of the Father, who draws all things together.

Bonaventure quotes Christ's statement: "I came forth from the Father, and have come into the world. Again I leave the world and go to the Father."[58] Similarly, observes Bonaventure, each one should say:

> *Domine, exivi a te summo, venio ad te summum et per te summum. Hoc est medium metaphysicum reducens, et haec est tota nostra metaphysica: de emanatione, de exemplaritate, de consummatione, scilicet illuminari per radios spirituales et reduci ad summum. Et sic eris verus metaphysicus.*[59]

In the dynamic movement of creation, the opposites of emanation and return coincide in the Word, who is the Alpha and the Omega. Thus in the Word is had the reconciliation of motion and rest, of eternity and time, of the static and the dynamic, of the flux of history and the solidity of the eternal forms, of process and the eternal ground, of the way out and the way back, of the way down and the way up. *Emanatio* and *reditus* are united in the Word; for he is the *persona media Trinitatis*, who is the means of the Father's outgoing self-expression and the return in the unity of the Spirit. Thus through its reflection of the Word as its exemplar, the entire cosmos shares the dynamic interpenetration of opposites of its Trinitarian archetype.

Although all the world shares in the coincidence of opposites, this is true of the human mind in a special way. First, the mind of man is turned as a mirror towards the external world, and in its knowing processes is related to the external world as subject to object, as microcosm to macrocosm. But man's mind is also a mirror turned upward to God. As image of God, man reflects God and is related to him with the polarity of subject to subject. In the realm of subjectivity there is a coincidence of interpenetration. God is more intimate to me that I am to myself. When I discovered his presence in me, or my presence in the divine mind, I realized what is most real about me. The *medium* of both of these types of coincidence of opposites is the Word himself. For he is the ground of the conformity between the objective structures of the external world and my own mind. As archetype of creation, he is the single source from which flow both the objective world and subjective mind. Hence, when I know with certitude, I grasp the objective structures of the external world in their unifying ground in the eternal Word. Thus the Word becomes the *medium* uniting the microcosm of my mind and the macrocosm of the external world. The Word is the 'interior teacher', illumining all minds. He is the changeless light that flashes in my mind when I grasp truth. Hence Bonaventure calls the Word truth itself:

> *Unde illud medium veritas est; et constat secundum Augustinum et alios Sanctos, quod "Christus habens cathedram in caelo docet interius"; nec aliquo modo aliqua veritas sciri potest nisi per illam veritatem.*[60]

In human knowledge the absolute and the relative, the changeable and the unchangeable, light and darkness coincide in a remarkable way. Only alluding to this in the first *Collatio in Hexaemeron*, Bonaventure develops it at greater length in the sermon *Christus, Unus Omnium Magister*. The human mind is changeable and fallible; truth is unchangeable and infallible. In the act of certain knowledge, we grasp the eternal, unchangeable, infallible truth, although we ourselves remain finite. While we do grasp the eternal light, we see now only in a glass darkly. What mediates this coincidence of opposites in knowledge? It is the uncreated Wisdom which is Christ: *"Talis autem lux non est intelligentiae creatae sed Sapientiae increatae, quae Christus est."*[61] Such a light is not the light of created intelligence but of uncreated Wisdom, which is Christ. Thus Bonaventure's doctrine of illumination is seen to contain the logic of the coincidence of opposites. Perhaps more than any other position of Bonaventure, his epistemology of illumination has suffered from being approached through discordant models. Frequently it is viewed either from a class model or an atomistic model and hence judged to lack an adequate foundation or logical coherence. We believe that by approaching Bonaventurian illumination through the model of the coincidence of opposites, one can see how it is grounded in the metaphysics of exemplarism and how it contains within itself a remarkable logical consistency.

Having seen the types of coincidence of opposites in creation, we turn now to the coincidence of opposites in the Incarnation and Redemption. In his Incarnation, Christ is the *medium physicum*, uniting the polar opposites of being: the highest and the lowest, the divine and matter—united through the microcosm of human nature in the hypostatic union.[62] By uniting the lowest to the highest, he brings the cosmos to the heights.[63] He becomes a center of radiating energy. Like the sun in the macrocosm and the human heart in the microcosm, he is an energizing center—the head of the mystical body, diffusing the energies of the Spirit throughout his members who are united to him. Thus as *medium physicum*, Christ is seen in his positive cosmic role: he brings the cosmos to its fullness by uniting the *maximum* and the *minimum* through the hypostatic union and he brings about the coincidence of the one and the many through his dynamic activity, sending out spiritual energy and uniting his members to himself.[64]

Bonaventure considers Christ the *medium mathematicum* in his crucifixion. As the mathematician measures the earth, which for the medievalist stood at the lowest level of the universe, so Christ plumbed the depths of earthly existence. Bonaventure is here expressing the kenotic aspect of the Redemption, in which the divinity empties itself assuming the form of a slave.[65] The Son of God became lowly, poor, insignificant. He took up our clay and went not merely to the surface of the earth, but to the depths of its center; for after his crucifixion he descended into hell and restored the heavenly dwellings.[66] Thus Christ becomes the coincidence of opposites uniting the heights and the depths. From a dynamic point of view, the opposites coincide; for the way down becomes the way up. By going to the depths of the earth, Christ unites the depths to the heights. Man had lost his center. Although as a mathematician he could measure other things, he could not measure himself. He had lost his center of balance; he had no fulcrum. Clouded with pride, he worked his own destruction. But Christ plunged into suffering on the cross; he cut through human pride and worked out man's salvation in the ashes of humility. Through the cross, Christ locates man's lost center. As Bonaventure says:

Medium enim, cum amissum
est in circulo
inveniri non potest nisi per duas
lineas se orthoganaliter
intersecantes.[67]

By going through the suffering of the cross, Christ reveals himself as the *medium logicum* in his resurrection. In the mystery of the cross, Christ confronts evil on its own grounds and comes away victorious. Bonaventure sees Christ confronting Satan in a type of cosmic *quaestio disputata*.[68] The opposites are joined, not in union but in combat. The two logics are opposed. Innocence confronts sin; good argues with evil. In the clash of good and evil, we see the most subtle and deceptive of the coincidence of opposites. For good and evil are related not as *maximum* and *minimum*, nor as microcosm—macrocosm, nor as complementaries—but rather as contraries: that is, evil is the negation of the good, but always retains an aspect of the good, although distorted, as its ontologicial foundation. Hence evil is the dark side of the good, or the shadow of the good. This is the basis for another coincidence of opposites: that of illusion and reality. Evil is deceptive; it appears to be good. It tempts one because it promises pleasure and benefits; but in reality, it brings the opposite—unhappiness and destruction. Hence Satan could use his deceptive logic on man. As his major premise he presupposed a true proposition: All men should desire to be like God because they are his image. But Satan's minor premise was false: If you eat, you will be like God. He promised life and gave death; he promised happiness and gave destruction. Man was overcome in his confrontation with Satan, for he was deceived by Satan's logic. Now Christ enters the debate; as ultimate reality and ultimate truth, Christ can deceive the deceiver and overcome the illusion of evil.

Christ becomes the middle term of a cosmic syllogism. Previously the extremes were not united; man and God were separated by sin. The word unites the extremes in his person through the hypostatic union, but this means that he must take up suffering and death. He must be similar to man if he is to make man similar to God. As Son of the Father, he possessed the divine nature, equal power and immortality. Yet as man he took up their opposites: suffering, weakness and death. But since he is Life itself, he leads humanity through death to life. Satan used the coincidence of opposites, promising life and giving death; Christ also used the coincidence of opposites, taking up death and pushing it to its ultimate to draw from it newness of life. Bonaventure describes Christ's logic as follows:

> *Major propositio fuit ab aeterno; sed assumtio in cruce; conclusio vero in resurrectione. Iudaei credebant Christum confudisse et improperabant ei: **Si Filius Dei es, descende de cruce**. Nam Christus non dicebat: sinite me vivere, sed dicebat: sinite me mortem assumere et alteri extremitati copulari, pati, mori; et tunc sequitur conclusio. Unde ipse illusit diabolo.*[69]

Having shattered the hold of evil, Christ can lead man on his return back to the Father. On the return Christ is first the *medium ethicum* in his ascension. Bonaventure uses the symbol of Moses' ascent of the mountain to illustrate the progress one should make in the life of virtue.[70] Having climbed from the foot of the mountain to its summit, man must stand before Christ as the Judge. Here Christ is the *medium iudiciale* or *politicum*, since he renders judgment and determines reward and punishment.[71] Finally, he is the *medium theologicum* in eternal happiness. For the Word is the *persona media* of the Trinity, and from him is derived all happiness.[72] Having begun from the Word as *persona media* in the Trinity, we return through this *medium*, which is also our goal. Here at the end of the cosmic process, we return to our source; the Omega is revealed as the Alpha; the end is the beginning.

As we look back over the cosmic vision painted in this *collatio*, we can see, first, several types of coincidence of opposites; secondly, that these are related in a dynamic way so as to become moments in an on-going process; thirdly, that Christ himself is the greatest coincidence of opposites, who integrates in himself all opposites and draws them to their completion and ultimate reconciliation.

In the Trinity we saw the coincidence of the static and dynamic: for the Word, as *persona media Trinitatis*, coincides with the Word as dynamic expression of the Father, through whom emanation and return are mediated in the Trinitarian life. Again it is through the Word that the coincidence of opposites is mediated in the mystery of creation. In the Word, in whom are produced the *rationes aeternae*, we have the ground for the union of the eternal and the temporal, the *maximum* and the *minimum*; and hence we have the metaphysical basis for Bonaventure's doctrine of exemplarism. Yet, from this point of view, exemplarism might appear static. However, the static aspect coincides with the dynamic, for the Word is also the Alpha and the Omega of the cosmic process. Just as the Trinitarian *emanatio* and *reditus* flowed through the Word, so the Word, as the *Ars Patris*, is the source of the emanation of temporal creation and, as divine Exemplar, he is the Omega drawing the comic process to its completion and return to the Father.

It is in the Word incarnate that creation reaches its highest perfection. For in Christ are united the polar opposites of divinity and matter in the microcosm of human nature. What appears as a union of static perfection becomes a cosmic force; for when Christ enters the cosmic process, he not only stands as the highest perfection on the scale of being, but also is a center of radiating energy drawing all things to himself. While, on the one hand, he brings the cosmos to its physical perfection, on the other, he has taken upon himself all the imperfections and suffering of a finite world burdened with sin. He has entered into the very depths of the universe, into the ashes of humility. But the way down paradoxically becomes the way up, for out of the destruction of death comes the glorified life of the resurrection. Since Christ has plunged into the depths of the struggle of the opposites of good and evil and emerged victorious, he can draw the cosmic process to its completion and bring man through a virtuous life and final judgment to eternal happiness.

Thus the *collatio* gives a striking view of Christ as the coincidence of opposites. This vision of Christ is not only rich in itself, but it can also provide a key to enter another level of Bonaventure's thought. Throughout his writing Bonaventure expresses himself on two levels simultaneously: (1) the theological-philosophical level, and (2) the level of religious symbols. One might look upon Bonaventure's use of symbols as mere literary devices to adorn his style; but such a judgment would not take into account the depth and power of his symbolic imagination and the intricate inter-relations of his symbols as they form a coherent pattern of their own and give structure and support to the theological-philosophical level. Thus for Bonaventure the symbol embodies a twofold coincidence of opposites. If we view the religious symbol on its own level, we see that it performs the function of theophany; for it attempts to manifest the divine in matter. Seen within Bonaventure's total thought, the symbol also unites matter and spirit, for it expresses on its own concrete level the theophanic vision that Bonaventure's theological and philosophical formulations are attempting the express. Thus the religious symbol becomes a microcosm for viewing the entire theological-philosophical structure of his thought. It is here that we see the Christological significance of religious symbols. The religious symbol is a microcosm pointing to Christ the macrocosm—who unites within himself the greatest possible coincidence of opposites. At this point we have returned to the position of Eliade with which we began our study:

One might even say that all hierophanies are simply prefigurations of the miracle of the Incarnation, that every hierophany is an abortive attempt to reveal the mystery of the coming together of God and man.[73]

This suggests a vast area for research in Bonaventure's thought. A mere glance at his symbols indicates that he uses the same type of religious symbol that both Eliade and Jung study in their respective research in comparative religion and in the psychology of religion.[74] For example, Bonaventure describes Christ as the *medium physicum*, the *medium mathematicum* and the *medium logicum*. If we take these notions together, we have a conception of Christ which corresponds to Eliade's concept of the *axis mundi*: the cosmic pillar linking the heavens, the earth and the underworld. This basic religious symbol is found throughout the world, both in primitive peoples and in developed cultures. It is at the core of the experience of hierophany and expresses a fundamental reconciliation of opposites. Eliade describes it as follows:

> This communication [between levels] is something expressed through the image of a universal pillar, *axis mundi*, which at once connects and supports heaven and earth and whose base is fixed in the world below (the infernal regions)… around this cosmic axis lies the world (= our world), hence the axis is located "in the middle," at the "navel of the earth;" it is the Center of the World.[75]

As the *medium physicum*, Christ stands at the center, linking God and creation. As the *axis mundi*, he is the center of the cosmos—radiating out to all the parts of the universe, like the sun in the macrocosm and the heart in the microcosm. Thus the two concepts of the cosmic pole and the cosmic center converge in Christ as the *medium physicum*. Yet as *medium mathematicum* and *medium logicum*, Christ goes not only to the surface of the earth, but to the underworld. He encounters evil and Satan. In the cosmic struggle between good and evil, he emerges victorious. He has entered into the depths of evil, has unmasked its deception, has transformed death to life and so restores the heavenly dwellings. Thus he becomes the *axis mundi* linking all levels of the universe.

The goal of Christ's work, according to Bonaventure, is to locate man's center, which has been lost by sin. This can be achieved only by two lines intersecting in the form of a cross. Bonaventure's image of the circle and the cross implies not only Eliade's concept of the *axis mundi* passing through the center of the universe, but in a special way recalls Jung's mandala symbol, which is the symbol of total integration. Jolande Jacobi summarizes Jung's concept of the mandala as follows:

Mandalas are among the oldest religious symbols of mankind; we have examples from as far back as the paleolithic age. They occur among all peoples and in all cultures, even in the form of sand paintings, as among the Pueblo Indians... We have also numerous mandalas from the Western Middle Ages and Renaissance, most of which show Christ at the center of the circle, surrounded by the four Evangelists or their symbols at the four cardinal points. . .

The mandalas all show the same typical arrangement and symmetry of the pictorial elements. Their basic design is a circle or square (most often a square) symbolizing 'wholeness', and in all of them the relation to a center is accentuated. Many have the form of a flower, a cross, or a wheel, and there is a distinct inclination toward the number four.[76]

Bonaventure's writing abounds in mandala symbols. A systematic study of these symbols would, we believe, yield a deeper understanding of the depth and power of his thought. Such a study is beyond the scope of our present enterprise, for it would require extended space and the integration of considerable material from psychology, literature, history and comparative religion. For our present purpose, we can merely point to Bonaventure's circle with the cross as a mandala symbol and note that it was intended by him to symbolize man's re-integration into spiritual totality after his disorientation of sin. Christ is seen as the great mathematician who restores psychic order— not by a simple external measurement, but by entering into the very depths of the cosmos to right its axes and to bring the human spirit to its center. This implies a finding of its midpoint, an integration of all its forces and a completion of its highest potential.

Although Christ as *axis mundi* has restored the cosmic harmony and has provided a mandala for the integration of the universe, each soul must go through the cosmic process on its return to the Father. Each must follow Christ as the *medium ethicum* in his ascent up the mountain. It is here that the symbols of the first *Collatio in Hexaemeron* converge with those of the *Itinerarium*. In the *Itinerarium* Bonaventure begins by recalling his own ascent up Mount Alverno and his meditation on the six-winged Seraph in the form of the Crucified, symbolizing both the way and the goal of the mind's ascent. Throughout the *Itinerarium* the ascent symbols blend into Christological symbols. The Seraph at the height of the mountain is in the form of the Crucified and at the center of the tabernacle we encounter the Mercy Seat, which is the symbol of Christ. Hence Christ is the way, the door, the ladder and the vehicle.[77]

Thus we see that while each religious symbol is itself a hierophany, it becomes a microcosm pointing to Christ, who as Image of the Father is the great symbol and as incarnate Word is the great hierophany—uniting opposites in an extraordinary way. For Bonaventure, as for Eliade and Jung, all religious symbols represent a *coincidentia oppositorum*, for symbols are themselves points where opposites converge. Furthermore, in Bonaventure's theophanic universe, where Christ is the great coincidence of opposites, all religious symbols are related to him as to their archetype. For the Christian, Christ is the great mandala symbol, representing the full differentiation of opposites, their dynamic process of development and their ultimate reconciliation in total integration. From the standpoint, then, of the coincidence of opposites, it is possible to see the logic and the coherence of the entire symbolic levels of Bonaventure's thought. Moreover, since both the theological-philosophical and the symbolic levels of his thought share in the structure and dynamics of the coincidence of opposites, it is possible to see how each supports and clarifies the other.

Seen against the background of Eliade's studies in the history of religions and Jung's studies of religious psychology, Bonaventure's thought reveals its enormous depth and richness. On the one hand, Eliade and Jung aid in our understanding of Bonaventure; but on the other, Bonaventure provides a concrete case of religious symbolism which brings to a high point of expression the very principles they propound. Bonaventure was a religious genius whose creative powers were in close touch with the archetypal religious symbols which are the heritage of men throughout the world. In this context, we can see the universal value of Bonaventure's thought and his relevance to our present age. For he not only draws richly upon universal religious symbols, but he provides an example of that fully developed and integral consciousness which is the goal of mankind. It is not by chance that mandala symbols emerge in his writings, for he embodies in his own person a high degree of differentiated opposites which are at the same time integrated into a multi-dimensional totality. And he points the way to others, at their own position in space and time in the cosmic process, to join with him in the return to the Father. For it is by the integration of all the opposites: of matter and spirit, of the eternal and the temporal, of the divine and the human, of death and life, of the resolution of the struggle of good and evil, that one reaches the height of the mountain and enters into the fullness of union.

In conclusion, we hope that our study has at least made a step towards verifying our hypothesis that the proper theoretical model for studying Bonaventure's thought is that of the *coincidentia oppositorum*. When one begins to analyze Bonaventure's thought from this point of view, he becomes aware of the extraordinary coherence of Bonaventure's vision. But he also becomes aware of its complexity. For Bonaventure does not explore one type of coincidence of opposites, but many types. And these types are themselves related as opposites. Thus there emerges an extraordinary dynamism, whose energy is felt throughout Bonaventure's thought. For the opposites are in constant polar tension, each energizing the other and each drawing the other into a type of Trinitarian emanation, interpenetration and return. Furthermore, an awareness of the central role of Christ as the great coincidence of opposites opens the door to a study of Bonaventure's religious symbolism. By seeing the religious symbol as a coincidence of opposites and as the microcosm pointing to Christ the macrocosm, we once again glimpse the extraordinary coherence and complexity of Bonaventure's thought. We believe, then, that the theoretical model of the   coincidence of opposites provides not only a logically consistent framework for the study of Bonaventure, but one which can be especially fruitful as an instrument of research.

Chapter 6
Francis of Assisi and Interreligious Dialogue

It is a great honor and pleasure for me to have been invited to deliver a plenary address to the distinguished scholars gathered here in Assisi to engage in interreligious dialogue. It is especially meaningful for me personally to speak here in Assisi on St. Francis and interreligious dialogue. For this occasion marks the meeting of two major paths I have taken in my academic and spiritual journeys. I first visited Assisi in 1961 as a tourist and a pilgrim, little realizing that within a year I would begin translating texts of the medieval Franciscan theologian Bonaventure. This led me to translate Bonaventure's biography of Francis and to explore over many years the spirituality, mysticism, and historical significance of Francis within the early Franciscan tradition.

This Franciscan journey was paralleled by another journey. Through the years as I did research on Bonaventure and Francis, I became increasingly involved in interreligious dialogue. My interest in other religions was awakened in 1954 when I was on an American Indian reservation near Topeka, Kansas, working with the Pottawatomie tribe, whose name means People of the Fire. I was fascinated to learn that their traditional religion was considered by the Vienna School of Ethnology to be one of the most archaic forms of religion surviving in the world. In a rudimentary way I began an interreligious dialogue with their leaders and extended this to the Sioux tribe on the Rosebud Reservation in South Dakota. This led me eventually to interreligious dialogue with Judaism, Islam, Hinduism, and other religions in various locations around the world.

These two journeys—into the world of Francis and into interreligious dialogue—have not been separate. They have constantly intersected, even interpenetrated. Each has thrown light on the other. It is this mutual enlightenment—in relation to our conference theme "God and God Equivalents"—that I hope to share with you in this present address.

Before I begin, I would like to tell you a story. Each of my visits to Assisi has been memorable, but my last was especially so for it highlighted in a new way Francis' connection with the world's religions. It was in August 1984, when my editor friend Richard Payne and I were traveling around the world contacting speakers for a major interreligious conference. In the course of that trip we had visited Buddhist temples in Kyoto and Bangkok, the sacred Hindu city of Varanasi, the Buddhist site at Sarnath, the great mosque in Delhi, and eventually Rome with its centuries of Christian history. From there we traveled to Assisi, and for the first time I experienced the city of St. Francis within the context of the holy cities of the world. I felt that Assisi had a rightful place among them and, in fact, could be best appreciated in the global perspective. During your days here perhaps you, too, will share my perception of Assisi which is summed up in the inscription at the threshold of the chapel of the Portiuncula at Sancta Maria degli Angeli: "Hic locus sanctus est" (This place is holy).

In my talk I would like to take you, in your imagination, on a tour of Assisi. Together we will visit sites where important events occurred in Francis' life—events that reveal the contributions he can make to interreligious dialogue. Our first stop will be the *vescovado*, or bishop's residence, where he stripped himself of his clothes before his father and the bishop, as a symbol of the life of poverty he was to embrace. The next stop will be at the convent of San Damiano, where he composed the *Canticle of Brother Sun*. The third will be some distance away, although depicted abundantly in art here in Assisi: Mount La Verna in Tuscany, where he has the climactic mystical experience of his life in a vision of a six-winged Seraph in the form of Christ crucified. Each event reveals his deep religious experience and inner attitudes which can be fruitfully transposed eight centuries later into the context of interreligious dialogue. Francis' message is not confined to Christianity. Like certain saints of other religions, he has something vital to say to our present era of global consciousness. In this sense he can be called a patron saint of interreligious dialogue.

Francis and Poverty

The life of Francis follows a classic pattern of the life of a saint: he had a religious awakening in early adulthood; a period of withdrawal, prayer and searching for the will of God; and the reception of divine guidance through inner enlightenment, dreams and visions. From hearing and reading certain Gospel texts, he received a clear understanding that he was to follow a lifestyle of radical poverty in imitation of Christ. Disciples gathered around him, and the little band walked to Rome, where Pope Innocent III gave official approval to their simple life of poverty. Thus began the Order of Friars Minor, or the Franciscan Order, as it is popularly known. Francis spent the next twenty years wandering through the villages of central Italy, preaching and healing the sick—all the while living a life of prayer, fasting, and other severe ascetical practices. Thousands joined his order—coming from all classes of society: knights and peasants, priests and laymen, scholars and the illiterate. His magnetism was irresistible: he was sensitive, charming, humanly attractive and at the same time endowed with great spiritual power that issued in countless miracles during his life and after his death. In 1224, two years before he died, he had the ecstatic vision of a six-winged Seraph in the form of Christ crucified, after which he received the stigmata, or the marks of Christ's wounds in his hands, feet, and side. Christians saw this as God's seal on the authenticity of his holiness and the life of poverty which he led. He died in 1226 near the chapel of the Portiuncula and two years later was officially canonized a saint by the Church. In 1230 the crypt of the Basilica of St. Francis in Assisi was completed and his body was moved there from the site of the Basilica of St. Clare, where it had been temporarily placed. Through the centuries Francis has been venerated as one of the most popular saints of the Catholic Church.

Poverty, along with humility, was central to his spirituality and to the order he founded. He was called *Il Poverello*, "the little poor man," and his order's title *Ordo Fratrum Minorum* (Order of the Lesser Brothers) suggests a fundamental attitude of humility. This Franciscan poverty is best symbolized by what happened at the bishop's residence, the first stop on our tour of Assisi. In the winter of 1206 the inhabitants of Assisi saw a crowd gathering at the residence of Bishop Guido. Francis, who was then in his mid-twenties, was in the process of leaving his father's home and embarking on a religious way of life. In his fervor he had taken cloth from his wealthy father's business, sold it in a nearby town, and had given the money to a poor priest to repair a church. Outraged, his father cast him in chains. After his mother released him, his father led him before the bishop to renounce his patrimony and return everything to him. In his biography of Francis, Bonaventure describes the scene:

> A true lover of poverty, Francis showed himself eager to comply; he went before the bishop without delaying or hesitating. He did not wait for any words nor did he speak any, but immediately took off his clothes and gave them back to his father... he even took off his underwear, stripping himself completely naked before all. He said to his father 'Until now I have called you father here on earth, but now I can say without reservation, Our Father who art in heaven (Matthew, 6:9), since I have placed all my treasure and hope in him.'[78]

Bonaventure reports that the bishop was amazed. Moved by Francis' fervor, he stood up and in tears embraced Francis, covering him with the mantle he was wearing. Bonaventure continues:

He bade his servants give Francis something to cover his body. They brought him a poor cheap cloak of a farmer who worked for the bishop. Francis accepted it gratefully and with his own hand marked a cross on it with a piece of chalk, thus designating it as the covering of a crucified man and a half-naked beggar.[79]

This image of the naked Francis became a symbol in Franciscan literature of his identification with the naked Christ, who died on the cross stripped of all possessions. Bonaventure comments on the scene: "Thus the servant of the Most High King was left naked so that he might follow his naked crucified Lord, whom he loved."[80] Francis himself carried out this symbolism further as his death approached. "He threw himself naked on the naked ground... naked he wished to go out of this world. He enjoined his friars assisting him, under obedience and charity, that when they saw he was dead, they should allow his body to lie naked on the ground for the length of time it takes to walk a leisurely mile."[81]

This image of nakedness symbolized for Francis the total stripping of himself. However, this image was balanced by another which expressed the spirit of joy and self-fulfillment with which he sought poverty. As he was beginning his religious journey, he told his friends that he had fallen in love with a beautiful lady whom he wished to marry.[82] Of course, his friends took this literally, but he meant it symbolically. The object of his love was, in fact, Lady Poverty. Through this allegory Francis channeled into his practice of renunciation the romantic energies that had been awakened in Europe in the twelfth century by the troubadour poets and the tellers of romantic tales. As a poet himself and a singer of songs, Francis shared this creative impulse which permeated his personality. The earliest Franciscan document, entitled *Sacrum Commercium*, written probably one year after his death is completely devoted to the allegory of Francis and his Lady Poverty, who is presented as Christ's widow, spurned by all suitors until the time of Francis.[83]

A century later it found its greatest artistic expression in one of the vaults over the altar of the lower church in the Basilica of St. Francis, attributed by tradition and some critics to Giotto. Here is depicted the marriage of Francis to Lady Poverty, who wears the traditional white of a bridal gown. But a close inspection reveals that her gown is torn and tattered and she is standing barefooted in brambles. Giotto's contemporary, the great epic poet Dante, combined the two basic Franciscan symbols of poverty in a most dramatic way. After telling the story of Francis' falling in love and marrying Lady Poverty, he recounts how Lady Poverty, who was first married to Christ, was present at his crucifixion. Yet she was closer to Christ there than even his mother, for while his mother stood below, she climbed on the cross herself to be with Christ in his death.[84]

Poverty and Interreligious Dialogue

What is the meaning of Francis' poverty for interreligious dialogue? Through poverty Francis embarked on the spiritual path of radical renunciation and asceticism, which links him with the ascetical and monastic traditions of Hinduism, Jainism, and Buddhism. His particular lifestyle of monasticism took the form of wandering beggar-preacher, who preached more by example than by words. In this he has thousands of counterparts in the East. Perhaps he is closest to the Jain monks, whose wandering is joined with a care for animals, birds, and insects which was a major characteristic of Francis. Moreover, nakedness plays a role in Jain monasticism.

It is possible to take Francis' poverty as a symbol for an attitude which is essential to interreligious dialogue. When a Christian and a Hindu, for example, enter into dialogue, their initial attitudes are crucial for its success. They may view each other's beliefs through the lens of their own. Such a perspective can create a distorted perception. On the other hand, they can, for a moment at least, strip themselves of their own worldview and with their faculty of empathy enter into the consciousness of the other, not only seeing the other's beliefs on their own terms, but also appreciating their religious value. This inner stripping can be symbolized by the exterior poverty of Francis and, in a similar way, the poverty of the monastic traditions of the world. Note that I spoke of stripping away for a moment; for if the stripping were permanent, it would undercut the basis of interreligious dialogue, namely, the deep commitment of the parties to their respective traditions. This stripping is temporary and functional in order to allow for an authentic grasping of the other's position. Once this is achieved, one returns to his or her own position, enriched and even transformed by contact with the other. As in the case of Francis, this stripping implies a deep humility; for if one begins dialogue from a superior stance, the creative mutual energies of dialogue will not be released but smothered.

This is a general observation. But what does Franciscan poverty have to say to the specific theme of our conference: "God and God-Equivalents"? In order to determine this, we must ask: What perception of God lies behind Francis' poverty? As we have seen, Francis identified with the poverty of Christ. The God of Francis is a God who empties himself, stripping himself of divinity in taking on human form. In his human existence, he empties himself even beyond normal human circumstances, taking upon himself humiliation, suffering, and death. Francis' God is a compassionate God whose loving-kindness expresses itself in concrete terms. Such a view of God has its counterparts in the *bhakti* traditions of Hinduism, with its incarnations of the divinity, in the divine attributes of mercy and compassion in Judaism and Islam, and in the similar God-equivalents in Buddhism: the Amida Buddha and the Bodhisattva. How these perceptions of God are related to the divine justice, transcendence, unknowability and emptiness are central matters of dialogue both within the traditions and among the traditions.

"The Canticle of Brother Sun"

On our tour of Assisi we now walk from the bishop's residence to the church of San Damiano, which is situated outside the city walls. This is the place where Francis, at the beginning of his religious conversion, heard the figure of Christ on the Cross say to him three times: "Francis, go and repair my house, which, as you see, is falling completely into ruin."[85] Taking the injunction literally, he set out to repair the church. Later God conveyed to him that it was the church as community of believers that Christ intended.

Seven years later, after his Order had been founded, he installed Clare of Assisi and her nuns in the convent of San Domiano, which became the mother house of the Poor Ladies, or the Poor Clares as they have been called, who constitute the female branch of the Franciscan Order. It was here in the spring of 1225, several months after he had received the stigmata, that he composed the *Canticle of Brother Sun*.

Let us proceed there in our imagination to the traditional spot of its composition, overlooking the convent garden and the vast plain that extends across the valley below Assisi. The details of its composition are recorded in the *Legenda Perugina*, one of the most authoritative early sources on the life of Francis. The text of the *Legenda* reads as follows:

St. Francis lay there [at San Damiano] for fifty days and could no longer see in the daytime the light of day, nor at night the light of the fire, but always remained in the house and in the little cell in darkness. Moreover, he had great pain in his eyes day and night so that at night he could scarcely rest or sleep, which was very bad for him and greatly aggravated the sickness of his eyes and his other infirmities. Also, if at any time he wished to rest or sleep, there were many mice in the house and in the little cell where he lay, which was a lean-to made of rushes attached to one side of the house. The mice ran backwards and forwards over him and around him, and so did not let him go to sleep. They even hindered him considerably at the time of prayer. Not only at night but even by day they so tormented him that even when he ate they got up on to the table, so that his companions and he himself considered it must be a temptation of the devil, as indeed it was.[86]

On one occasion Francis was so tormented by these sufferings that he prayed to God in his distress, as the *Legenda* tells us: "One night St. Francis was thinking about how many tribulations he had and began to feel sorry for himself, saying inwardly: "Lord, come to my help and look on my infirmities so that I may be able to bear them patiently."[87]

At this point he heard God speak within himself, promising him eternal happiness in the kingdom of heaven. However God did not merely state this gift directly but expressed it through the image of the earth transformed into gold:

> Immediately it was said to him in spirit: 'Tell me, brother: if anyone were to give you for your infirmities and tribulations such a great and precious treasure that, if the whole earth were pure gold, all stones were precious stones, and all water were balsam, yet you would consider all this as nothing, and these substances as earth, stones, and water in comparison with the great and precious treasure given to you, surely you would rejoice greatly?[88]

The *Legenda* continues:

> St. Francis replied: 'That would be a great treasure, Lord, and worth the seeking, truly precious and greatly to be loved and desired.' He said to him: 'Therefore, brother, rejoice, and rather be glad in your infirmities and tribulations, since henceforth you are as secure as if you were already in my kingdom.'[89]

According to the text, when Francis arose in the morning, he told his companions of the assurance God had given him and how he should rejoice and give thanks to him. The text continues:

> 'Therefore I want for his praise and my consolation, and the edification of our neighbors, to make a new song of Praise of the Lord for his creatures, which we use daily and without which we could not live. In them the human race greatly offends the Creator and daily we are ungrateful for such grace, because we do not praise our creator and giver of all good things which we ought.' Sitting down, he began to meditate and afterwards began: 'Altissimo, omnipotente, bon Signore.'

He made a song on the creatures and taught his companions to recite it.[90]

Francis composed his canticle in the Umbrian dialect of medieval Italian. The Umbrian text is given below, followed by an English translation.[91] On this occasion, Francis also composed a melody which has not been preserved, although the oldest manuscript has provided space for musical notations, which were not recorded.

Il Cantico Di Frate Sole

1 Altissimu onnipotente bon signore
2 Tue so le laude, la gloria e l'onore et onne benedictione.
3 Ad te solo, altissimo, se konfano,
4 Et nullu homo ene dignu te mentovare.

5 Laudato sie, mi signore, cun tucte le tue creature,
6 Spetialmente messor lo frate sole,
7 Lo qual'è iorno, et allumini noi per loi.
8 Et ellu è bellu e radiante con grande splendore,
9 De te, altissimo, porta significatione.

10 Laudato si, mi signore, per sora luna e le stelle,
11 In celu l'ài formate clarite et pretiose et belle.
12 Laudato si, mi signore, pre frate vento,
13 Et per aere et nubil et sereno et omne tempo,
14 Per lo quale al e tue creature dai sustentamento.

15 Laudato si, mi signore, per sor aqua,
16 La quale è multo utile et humile et pretiosa et casta.
17 Laudato si, mi signore, per frate focu,
18 Per lo quale enn' allumini la nocte,
19 Ed ello è bello et iocundo et robustoso et forte.

20 Laudato si, mi signore, per sora nostra matre terre,
21 La quale ne sustenta et governa,
22 Et produce diversi fructi con coloriti flori et herba.
23 Laudato si, mi signore, per quelli ke perdonano per lo tuo amore,
24 Et sostengo infirmitate et tribulatione.
25 Beati quelli ke 'l sosterrano in pace,

26 Ka da te, altissimo, sirano incoronati.
27 Laudato si, mi signore, per sora nostra morte corporale,
28 Da la quale nullu homo vivente po' skappare.
29 Guai a quelli, ke morrano ne la peccata mortali:
30 Beati quelli ke travarà ne le tue santissime voluntati,

31 Ka la morte secunda nol farrà male.
32 Laudate et benedicete mi signore,
33 Et rengratiate et serviateli cun grande humilitate.

The Canticle of Brother Sun

1   Most high omnipotent good Lord,
2   Yours are the praises, the glory, the honor and all blessing.
3   To you alone, Most High, do they belong,
4   And no man is worthy to mention you.
5   Praised be you, my Lord, with all your creatures,

6   Especially Sir Brother Sun,
7   Who makes the day and through whom you give us light.
8   And he is beautiful and radiant with great splendor,
9   And bears the signification of you, Most High One.
10 Praised be you, my Lord, for Sister Moon and the stars,

11 You have formed them in heaven clear and precious and beautiful.
12 Praised be you, my Lord, for Brother Wind,
13 And for the air—cloudy and serene—and every kind of weather,
14 By which you give sustenance to your creatures.
15 Praised be you, my Lord, for Sister Water,

16 Which is very useful and humble and precious and chaste.
17 Praised be you, my Lord, for Brother Fire,
18 By whom you light the night,
19 And he is beautiful and jocund and robust and strong.
20 Praised be you, my Lord, for our sister Mother Earth,

21 Who sustains and governs us,
22 And produces various fruits with colored flowers and herbs.
23 Praised be you, my Lord, for those who give pardon for your love

24 and bear infirmity and tribulation,
25 Blessed are those who endure in peace,

26 For by you, Most High, they will be crowned.
27 Praised be you, Lord, for our Sister Bodily Death,
28 From whom no living man can escape.
29 Woe to those who die in mortal sin.
30 Blessed are those whom death will find in your most holy will,

31 For the second death shall do them no harm.
32 Praise and bless my Lord and give him thanks
33 And serve him with great humility.

The Canticle and Interreligious Dialogue

What is the significance of Francis' canticle for interreligious dialogue? It provides one of the most classical expressions of the immanence of God in creation within the Christian tradition. In so doing, it resonates with similar expressions in Judaism, especially Psalm 148 and "The Canticle of The Three Young Men" in the Book of Daniel (3:52-90), which undoubtedly influenced Francis. It has similarities with themes in the Koran, and in the theistic strands of Hinduism as well as with God-equivalents in Taoism and Buddhism. On this and other points, there is a remarkable similarity between Francis and archaic religions.

If we turn to Bonaventure, we can see another dimension of Francis' experience of God which provides further connections with the world's religions. A great philosopher and theologian in his own right, Bonaventure situated Francis' experience of the immanence of God in creation within the already elaborated Christian Neoplatonic tradition.[92] Like Augustine and the Pseudo-Dionysius before him, Bonaventure saw all creation emanating from God, reflecting God, and returning to God. This is based on the Christian doctrine of the Trinity, in which the Father is seen as the fountain fullness (*fontalis plenitudo*) of the divinity. Out of his boundless fecundity, the Father generates the Son and in the Son the divine archetypes or ideas of all he can make. The emanation within the Trinity is completed in the spiration of the Holy Spirit, who is the love and unity of the Father and the Son.

If the divinity decides to create a world in space and time, this act begins with the Father's fecundity and proceeds through the Son, who is the exemplar of all the forms in the phenomenal world, and is completed in the

Holy Spirit, who draws creation back to its source. Thus the world is a vast mirror reflecting God. It is like a stained-glass window in a Gothic cathedral: the divine light shines through creatures thus refracting the divine manifestation in a myriad of shapes and colors. This theological-philosophical system has similarities in the Neoplatonic strands of Judaism and Islam, as well as in the emanation traditions of Hinduism and Buddhism. Bonaventure has a counterpart in the Hindu theologian Râmânuja, whose qualified non-dualism corresponds with Bonaventure's Franciscanism on a number of specific points.[93]

Francis' canticle can also throw light on the process of interreligious dialogue. There is a close connection between his radical poverty and his experience in the presence of God in creation. By detaching himself from material possessions, he removes the opaqueness of his ego to allow the presence of God to shine through the world. This is expressed beautifully in the *Sacrum Commercium*, when Francis and his friars climb a mountain to visit Lady Poverty. She asks them to showed her their cloister—a reference to the elaborate Benedictine monasteries. Taking her to a certain hill, they show her the whole world, as far as she could see, and said: "This, Lady, is our cloister."[94] Having liberated themselves from attachment, they now possess the entire world in its deeper sense containing the presence of God. We can carry further the symbolism of poverty to the fullness that can emerge in interreligious dialogue. The temporary stripping of our own worldviews can allow us to enter the worldviews of others where we can be enriched by the values we discover there. Like Francis, then, we can sing a new canticle, rejoicing in the varieties of religious experience, of wisdom, of spiritual paths— just as he rejoiced in the varieties of creatures.

The Seraph and Interreligious Dialogue

We will now travel to the third site on our Franciscan journey: the mountain of La Verna in Tuscany, directly east of Florence. This is indeed a holy mountain, a massive form, with a rocky wall near the summit, standing alone among the Apennines, stark, wild, and deserted even to this day. In 1224, two years before his death, Francis was spending several weeks there in prayer and fasting. In this setting he had a visionary mystical experience which was the climax of his religious life. Immediately after this vision Francis received the stigmata. Bonaventure describes the scene:

On a certain morning about the Feast of the Exaltation of the Cross [September 14], while Francis was praying on the mountainside, he saw a Seraph with six fiery and shining wings descend from the height of heaven. And when in swift flight the Seraph had reached a spot in the air near the man of God, there appeared between the wings the figure of a man crucified, with his hands and feet extended in the form of a cross and fastened to a cross. Two of the wings were lifted above his head, two were extended for flight and two covered his whole body. When Francis saw this, he was overwhelmed and his heart was flooded with a mixture of joy and sorrow. He rejoiced because of the gracious way Christ looked upon him under the appearance of the Seraph, but the fact that he was fastened to a cross pierced his soul with a sword of compassionate sorrow. (Luke 2:35) [95]

This was the most celebrated Christian mystical experience of the Middle Ages. Bonaventure saw it as the symbol of the soul's journey into God. It was depicted in art countless times, for example, by Giotto and his school, as can be seen in the Basilica of St. Francis here in Assisi.

What does it mean for interreligious dialogue and the theme of our conference? Bonaventure interpreted it as the highest experience of God as love. In the Middle Ages the fiery wings of the Seraph symbolized the fire of the love of God. In Francis' experience this included both God's love for Francis and his love for God and, most eminently, God himself as love. In the seventh chapter of his *Soul's Journey into God*, which is based on this vision, Bonaventure describes "the fire that totally inflames and carries us into God by ecstatic unctions and burning affections. This fire is God and *his furnace is in Jerusalem.*" (Isaiah 31:9) [96]

For Francis and—following him—the entire Franciscan tradition, God is love. This resonates with the spiritual paths of love in the other religions, for example the *bhakti* tradition of Hinduism, the *Zohar* in Judaism, and the mystical love poetry of Islam. This raises the question: How is this related to the spiritual path of knowledge and the mystical experience of God as light and Truth, or to the path of negation and the mystical experience of God as emptiness? All of these are found in Christianity as well as in other religions. Francis offers us a striking example of experiencing God as love, but leaves to others—at this conference to us—to explore the answer to this question.

We have been examining here Francis' ecstatic mystical experience of God as love, but there is manifested in his vision another form of love: compassion for the suffering of Christ in his humanity. Bonaventure highlights this when he says: "When Francis saw this, he was overwhelmed and his heart was flooded with a mixture of joy and sorrow. He rejoiced because of the gracious way Christ looked upon him under the appearance of the Seraph, but the fact that he was fastened to a cross *pierced his soul with a sword of compassionate sorrow*." (Luke 2:35) [97] I have indicated above the relation of Francis' compassion to other religions. What I would like to highlight here is the coincidence of opposites in Francis' mysticism: the coincidence of joy and sorrow. I believe that the coincidence of opposites permeates the experience of Francis and the thought of Bonaventure—a coincidence of opposites that one can find in the other religions as well. To explore this, I believe, would throw much light on interreligious dialogue and our conference theme. [98]

Our visit to La Verna brings to a close our tour of Franciscan sites. It also brings to completion the model of interreligious dialogue I have been drawing from the events in Francis' life. We began with the temporary stripping of our worldview to allow us the freedom to empathize with the worldview of others. It moved into the positive experience of the varieties of religious consciousness in the other traditions, as Francis rejoiced in the varieties of creatures as manifestations of God. Finally, as symbolized by La Verna, it reached its climax in a coincidence of opposites whereby we appropriate into our own worldview the richness we have discovered from dialogue with others. And with Francis we return to continue the process, drawn by the compassion that links us to the world community as we proceed through interreligious dialogue in our common spiritual journey.

Through history Francis has been a sign of peace. As Bonaventure recalls: "At the beginning and the end of every sermon he announced peace; in every greeting he wished for peace; in every contemplation he sighed for ecstatic peace."[99] What better way to close this talk but with Francis' own wish for peace, which has become the motto of the Franciscan order: Pax and Bonum— Peace and Goodness!

Chapter 7
Cross-Cultural Research:
Hindu and Christian

Meister Eckhart has played a central role in two major areas of religious concern in the 20th century: the study of Christian mysticism and the dialogue of world religions. A glance at the programs of the Kalamazoo conference over the past several years reveals an increasing interest in mysticism and the prominent place that Eckhart has had in this development. Recent translations of Eckhart and scholarly studies confirm this trend. Parallel with this is the role that he has played in the encounter of East and West. It is Eckhart who is singled out as the Christian partner in dialogue with Buddhism, particularly Zen, and with Hinduism in its non-dualist form of Vedanta. The classic study in the latter area is Rudolf Otto's *Mysticism East and West*, which compares and contrasts Eckhart with the great medieval Hindu theologian Sánkara.[100]

Within the context of these two trends, I would like to describe a research project on Eckhart that I am engaged in at the present time. In this study I focus upon the method of research employed in the project—namely phenomenology. Since the method is being employed in a cross-cultural context, this study uses the word "transcultural." The prefix "trans" is understood in its basic horizontal sense of "across" rather than the vertical sense of "above." Hence the title of the paper refers to cross-cultural phenomenology, not phenomenology above and beyond culture.

Cross-Cultural Research Project

My own work over the past several years has focused on the study of Christian mysticism within its own historical context and in dialogue with world religions. From 1978 until 1984 I participated in a research seminar organized by Peter Berger, the sociologist of religion, on mysticism in world religions. Some ten to fifteen specialists met about five times a year, first in New York and then in Boston, to explore mystical experiences in Hinduism, Buddhism, Judaism, Christianity and Islam, both on their own terms and in comparison among themselves.

Although much clarification issued from this research, I felt it was necessary to supplement it by a more controlled project, using a common methodology whose presuppositions would be brought to light at the outset. On a trip to India in 1983 I met Professor R. Balasubramanian, director of the

Dr. S. Radhakrishnan Institute for Advanced Study in Philosophy of the University of Madras. I discovered that he had been using in his study of Hindu mysticism the same method—phenomenology—that I had been using to study Christian mysticism. So I proposed that we collaborate on a joint project in the cross-cultural, interreligious study of mysticism from which would come a book entitled *Mysticism: Hindu and Christian.* He would write chapters on Râmânuja and Sánkara, and I would do chapters on Bonaventure and Eckhart. We would agree in the introduction on a common methodology and collaborate on a conclusion. He accepted and invited me to deliver five lectures at the University of Madras in January, 1984. During these talks, I laid out my position on method and applied it to Bonaventure and Eckhart; then we had a dialogue on their relation to Râmânuja and Sánkara. [101]   He agreed with my presentation of the method to the point of saying that we could work out a statement of method in our first chapter to which both of us would sign our names. He invited me back to give three more lectures at the University of Madras in 1985, and I invited him to New York for a month in the fall of 1985, during which time we hoped to advance our project substantially.

This project is in the tradition of Rudolph Otto's book, *Mysticism East and West,* but differs on major points. Instead of a Western scholar studying a Hindu and a Christian mystic, we have two scholars, one from an Indian Hindu background. Such a configuration has many advantages, since it is more likely than Otto's approach to be authentically in touch with the Hindu materials. Furthermore, it reflects the present climate of cross-cultural studies of religion, which is more dialogic and interreligious than in Otto's generation, as is witnessed by the cross-cultural representation in Peter Berger's seminar. It begins by clarifying a common method and examining critically its cross-cultural dimensions. Of course, Otto's book, *The Idea of the Holy,* which uses phenomenology, could be looked upon as supplying this statement of method, but it is not specifically oriented to cross-cultural studies. [102]

Methodology for Mysticism

The method I have proposed to Prof. Balasubramanian is akin to the phenomenology of Edmund Husserl, in that it proceeds by describing the contents of consciousness. However, it does not bracket and hold in abeyance the metaphysical content of the consciousness it is studying, although the observer may be called upon to bracket his own metaphysical presuppositions. Nor does the method adopt the model in which all intellectual content is derived from the interpretation of raw experience by subjective consciousness. On the contrary, this method is open to the possibility that the intellectual content of the experience can come from the very object of consciousness.

I propose the following as stages of a journey into the study of mystical consciousness:

The first stage is to encounter mystical consciousness. This may be a personal experience of the investigator that is reflected on later. Or it may be the experience of another that is described to the investigator, either personally by the subject or through writings. The investigator might even be present during the mystical experience of the subject or learn of it later. Or in the usual academic context, the investigator studies classical texts. Even here there is a variety of genres. Some mystical writings recount personal experience, for example, those of Augustine, Bernard of Clairvaux and Julian of Norwich. Others record the experience through a biographer—like the ecstatic experience of Francis of Assisi, when he received the stigmata. Or they may be works giving instruction on the stages of mystical contemplation, for example, Bonaventure's *The Soul's Journey into God*, or sermons like Eckhart's, intended to evoke in the listener levels of contemplative and mystical consciousness.

The second stage of the method is to enter into the consciousness of the mystic. This may seem impossible. Certain philosophical positions take a radically solipsistic stance, claiming that we can know only the contents of our own consciousness, and certainly that we cannot know the internal contents of another person's consciousness. This problem is compounded by the fact that we are not dealing here with everyday forms of consciousness, for example, of a tree or a hat, which we all can easily share, but rather altered states of consciousness that are contemplative or even ecstatic. How is it possible for us to share this experience? I believe that we can, through the capacity for empathy that we all have, and that some have cultivated to a high degree. If we hold, as I do, that we all have the capacity for contemplative and mystical experience, then we can have a spontaneous resonance with even high levels of mystical consciousness. And by our capacity for empathy, we can enter at least to some extent, into the consciousness of another, even of a mystic.

The third stage of the method involves describing the contents of consciousness of the mystic. Many elements fall within this stage: for example, in the case of nature mysticism, the mystic's experience of sense objects or the universe as a whole. I would like to focus here on one, a distinctive and crucial dimension: that of the divine, absolute reality. I realize that I am speaking of a specific type of mysticism, namely, God mysticism or theistic mysticism. However, I do not want to take theism in a narrow sense of a personal God, but of absolute reality, differing in ontological status from all other things and designated in some positive or affirmative fashion, not merely by silence or negative judgments. I will deal with the problem of negative and positive approaches later. The point I wish to make here is that the ontological status of this reality must be taken into account seriously in dealing with the mystical experience.

I propose that intentionality is the perspective from which to view mystical experience. Husserlian phenomenology drew the Aristotelian notion of the intentionality of consciousness from Franz Brentano. According to intentionality, our consciousness "intends," in the Latin etymological root meaning of "stretching toward" an object. It is consciousness of something.

What is the intentionality of God mysticism? What is the object of consciousness? I claim that it is the reality of the divine—with all the divine attributes that the classical theologies have affirmed. This ontological affirmation cannot be bracketed, nor can it be said to be merely the mystic's subjective interpretation. What makes God mysticism, what constitutes its distinctive character, is precisely the experience of God as the real, as that which is. This is not a mere interpretation of the experience; it constitutes the very essence of the experience.

Intentionality also can help answer the question that has been recently raised again by Steven Katz and others: Is there one form of mystical experience or many?[103] I believe that there has been a lack of critical reflection in posing the question, which has been formulated in terms derived from the finite realm of multiplicity. Instead, if it is explored through the very intentionality of God mysticism, then the ontological status of the object—the unique divinity— can provide the basis for the claim of unity. If God is perceived as being the one without a second, then, when mystics touch that reality, they realize that they have reached the same realm that all other God mystics have reached. In this sense, at least, there is only one experience of the divine, since the divine is the uniquely one, although there may be diversities in the subjective paths, and even among the divine attributes. But even in the diversity of the divine attributes, the mystics perceive the divine nature, which is the point where the intentionality of their experience converges.

Eckhart's Desert of the Godhead

Let us now apply this phenomenological method to Eckhart's desert of the Godhead. In his celebrated sermon on the theme "Blessed are the poor in spirit," Eckhart moves toward the desert of the Godhead by a radical detachment. He distinguishes two kinds of poverty: external and internal. After glossing over external poverty, which he approves, he directs his attention to internal poverty. "A poor man," he says, "wants nothing, and knows nothing, and has nothing." He points out how "people say that a man is poor who wants nothing; but they interpret it in this way, that a man ought to live so that he never fulfills his own will in anything, but that he ought to comfort himself so that he may fulfill God's dearest will." But Eckhart says that such are not poor men. "If a person wants really to have poverty," he says, "he ought to be as free of his own created will as he was when he did not exist." He goes on to say: "So long as you have a will to fulfill God's will, and a longing for God and for eternity, then you are not poor; for a poor man is one who has a will and a longing for nothing."[104]

Eckhart then proceeds in his radical analysis, saying that we must be free from God himself. He speaks of his existence in the first cause, saying that there he had no 'God:' "I wanted nothing, I longed for nothing, for I was an empty being.... But when I went out from my own free will and received my created being, then I had a 'God,' for before there were any creatures, God was not 'God,' but he was what he was." He concludes: "So let us pray to God that we may be free of 'God,' and that we may apprehend and rejoice in that everlasting truth in which the highest angel and the fly and the soul are equal— there where I was established, where I wanted what I was, and was what I wanted."[105]

Stripped of God, Eckhart enters into the desert of the Godhead, where there is no differentiation, no distinction:

> I speak in all truth, truth that is eternal and enduring, that this same light [the spark of the soul] is not content with the simple divine essence in its repose, as it neither gives nor receives; but it wants to know the source of this essence, it wants to go into the simple ground, into the quiet desert, into which distinction never gazed, nor the Father, nor the Son, nor the Holy Spirit.[106]

In another passage, Eckhart evokes the same experience:

> But if all images are detached from the soul, and it contemplates only the Simple One, then the soul's naked being finds the naked, formless being of the divine unity, which is there a being above being, accepting and reposing in itself. Ah, marvel of marvels, how noble is that acceptance, when the soul's being can accept nothing else than the naked unity of God![107]

Applying the phenomenological method to Eckhart's experience of the desert of the Godhead, we can ask: What is the intentionality of his consciousness? What his consciousness tends toward is the emptiness of the Godhead—beyond the divine attributes, beyond the persons of the Trinity. It is the Godhead stripped of all positive perfections: the naked absolute. Note that this consciousness is already on the level of the divine; it is not merely a negation of creatures, a negation of finitude, a negation of the superficial self. It has moved beyond the horizon of finitude, beyond God as Truth and Goodness into the divine abyss.

I believe that when Eckhart strips himself of God and ventures into the desert, he does not leave the realm of the ontologically divine. What he strips away is not the divinity itself, but its determinate dimension. If this were not the case, then the desert of the Godhead would collapse into the prime matter of Aristotle. If the intentionality of the experience remained on the level of the ontologically finite, then he would merely strip away finite forms and plunge into the undifferentiated potentiality of the lowest stratum of reality: prime matter. The intentionality of a mystical experience of prime matter (I believe such an experience is possible) would be poles apart from Eckhart's desert of the Godhead. In the desert all differentiations disappear, not because they are absorbed into their substrate, but because we have reached an ontological realm of the divine that is prior to its determinate attributes, prior to the Father's power to generate, prior to his determinate Logos, with its storehouse of determinate divine ideas.

Such a phenomenological clarification provides the basis for understanding the internal coherence of Eckhart's mysticism. He affirms also the Trinity and the determinate divine attributes; for these, too, are on the level of the ontological divine. If we had time to explore this further, we could see that the desert and the Trinity are related according to the coincidence of opposites of mutually affirming complementarity.[108]

What does this offer for a dialogue with Sánkara, who on this matter is strikingly close to the Dominican? There is much evidence to support the conclusion that Sánkara's experience of Brahman, beyond all differentiations, has the same intentionality as that of Eckhart's desert of the divinity. It is precisely Brahman's ontological divinity that makes Sankára proclaim that only Brahman is and that all else is illusory. It is this intentionality which, among other things, Dr. Balasubramanian and I will attempt to study further cross-culturally, employing a common method of phenomenology. Perhaps next year I can report on our results.

Chapter 8
States of Consciousness:
Charting the Mystical Path

The twentieth century has witnessed two remarkable breakthroughs into the inner realms of the human psyche. After several centuries of exploring the outer structures of the universe through empirical science, Western thinkers opened the door of the psyche and began exploring the dynamics of the unconscious. In the early years of this century, Freud and Jung led the expedition of psychotherapy that ushered in a new Age of Discovery of the inner world of the psyche.

Later in the century a similar breakthrough took place in religion. On this occasion the voyage of discovery was led by spiritual teachers from the East who came to the United States in the 1950s and 1960s. Under their guidance Westerners, who had been weighed down by materialism, were awakened to deeper values and began to explore the inner world of the human spirit. Rather than focusing on objective formulas of belief and the institutional structures of religion, they turned to the inner heart and soul of religion, the realm that had been cultivated by ancient spiritual wisdom. This was not merely a turn to subjective religious experience. It was much deeper, for like psychotherapy, it brought to light a process of growth and development at a deep level of the psyche, a process that had been described in classical texts as a spiritual journey. Many realized that these two breakthroughs were touching common ground in the psyche. Yet the boundaries were not clear. Where do they overlap and interpenetrate? Where do they diverge? After some thirty years, these questions are still with us today. How is psychotherapy related to the classical traditions of spirituality? This remains one of the most challenging issues of our time.

The encounter of psychotherapy and spirituality has been complex in itself, but it has been compounded by the way in which spirituality has emerged since the 1960s.[109] After the invasion of the gurus and Zen masters, Jews and Christians in the 1970s began to search for their own spiritual roots. This process of assimilation of their past is still going on. As it continues, we can observe a more sophisticated dialogue between these two traditions and psychotherapy. At the same time there has been a rapid assimilation of Buddhist and Hindu spirituality by various forms of psychotherapy. Often the assimilation has been pursued without relating the Buddhist and Hindu components to classical Jewish and Christian elements.

Meanwhile another process is taking place, not immediately related to psychotherapy, namely, the increasing interaction of the classical spiritual traditions of the world among themselves through interreligious dialogue. As a result of this encounter, I believe there is emerging a comprehensive and multidimensional spiritual wisdom of the world's religions, which can be called a world spirituality.[110] This emerging world spirituality has already begun to affect the dialogue between spirituality and psychotherapy by enlarging the spiritual horizons of the psyche. But to add further complications, this emerging world spirituality is not static. At the very time when it is surfacing, world spirituality itself is being transformed by forces that are also affecting psychotherapy.[111] In fact, it is my opinion that psychotherapy can give us a privileged clue to understand this transformation.

Against this background I will highlight certain themes that I hope will clarify the relation between spirituality and psychotherapy. I will begin by presenting a definition of spirituality and then link it to the theme of the conference by quoting Augustine and other spiritual teachers on the role of desire in the spiritual quest as it unfolds in various maps of the spiritual journey. Then, from research in altered states of consciousness I will outline a model for relating spirituality and psychotherapy. I will close by highlighting certain new directions in spirituality that might bring about closer contact with psychotherapy.

Definition of Spirituality

At this point I would like to propose, at least as a working definition of spirituality, a statement taken from a communication that was sent in 1981 to the editors of the twenty-five-volume series *World Spirituality: An Encyclopedic History of the Religious Quest*, of which I have the privilege of being general editor. Published by the Crossroads Publishing Company, this series attempts to present the accumulated spiritual wisdom of the human community in its historical unfolding.[112] It deals with the spirituality of primal peoples, the major religions—Hindu, Buddhist, Taoist, Confucianist, Jewish, Christian and Islamic—as well as other traditions. Its later volumes treat the encounter of spiritualities, past, present and future. I cite this description for several reasons: it emerges out of one of the most significant current attempts in the academic study of religion to describe spirituality; it seeks to be universal in that it was proposed to some five hundred contributors from the major traditions around the world to guide them as they write articles on the wide range of spirituality; since it is formulated from the standpoint of the interiority of the human person, it has immediate resonance with psychotherapy. Because it was designed for Buddhists as well as theists, the terms "God" and "divine" were not used, although they are implied for theistic traditions. I would like to state that those working on the project do not consider this statement "the last word" on the subject, but just one of many possible formulations from a number of contemporary perspectives. The statement reads as follows:

> The series focuses on that inner dimension of the person called by certain traditions "the spirit." This spiritual core is the deepest center of the person. It is here that the person is open to a transcendent dimension; it is here that the person experiences ultimate reality. The series will explore the discovery of this core, the dynamics of its development and its journey to the ultimate goal. It will deal with prayer, spiritual direction, the various maps of the spiritual journey and the methods of advancement in the spiritual ascent.[113]

Note the focus on the spiritual core as the deepest center of the person, where the person is open to a transcendent dimension. How does this relate to the concept of the person in psychotherapy? Note also the discovery and activation of this core and its journey to the ultimate goal. How does this relate to the beginning of the therapeutic process and the stages of its journey? I will return to these questions later.

Before leaving this statement, I would like to make an observation on the relation of spirituality to mysticism. As used at present in the academic community, the two terms overlap but at the same time reflect positions along a spectrum of experience. "Spirituality" has the broader scope, with the term "mysticism" denoting moments along the journey when a person experiences the transcendent with an ecstatic or rapturous intensity of consciousness.

The Fires of Desire

In the light of the above definition of spirituality, I would like to cite examples from spiritual and mystical writings dealing with the fires of desire in the religious quest. These texts can be seen as articulating the passionate desire that bursts from the spiritual core of the person and draws his soul to union with the divine Beloved. At the very outset of his *Confessions*, Augustine exclaims to God: "You have made us for yourself, and our heart is restless until it rests in you."[114] The remainder of his book spells out Augustine's anguishing search for God along the spiritual path of wisdom or knowledge. His search reaches its goal in an ecstatic mystical experience in which he encounters God as light in the depths of his soul.

Having traveled to Milan, he fell in with a circle of Christian Platonists who had gathered around Bishop Ambrose. In that context, he read the books of the Platonists. Directed by this reading, he tells us, he entered into his inmost being (*in intima mea*). This he could do, he says, because God was his guide. "I entered there, and by my soul's eye such as it was, I saw above that same eye of my soul, above my mind, an unchangeable light." This was no ordinary light, such as we perceive with our senses, nor was it "a greater light, as it were, of the same kind, as though that light would shine many, many times more bright, and by its great power to fill the whole universe. Not such was that light, but different, far different from all other lights." Augustine claims it was on a different ontological level: "Nor was it above my mind, as oil is above water, or as sky above earth. It was above my mind, because it made me, and I was beneath it because I was made by it." He then identifies the light as God: "He who knows truth, knows that light, and he who knows it knows eternity. Love knows it. O eternal truth, and true love and beloved eternity! You are my God, and I sigh for you day and night!"[115]

Augustine is an interesting case study for issues at hand. The *Confessions* illustrate our definition of spirituality, with the awakening of spiritual desire that drew him on a circuitous journey, which could be interpreted from a Freudian and a Jungian perspective. Yet it culminates in a mystical experience that, at face value, seems to stand outside the Freudian or Jungian horizons of the psyche. How are the Freudian and Jungian levels related to his spiritual journey? Were they dimensions of a deeper spiritual process? And how was the mystical experience of God as light related to the Freudian and Jungian antecedents?

These questions emerge from the works of other spiritual writers. For example, Bernard of Clairvaux leads the reader on a spiritual journey that begins, proceeds, and ends with the passionate love that the soul has for its Beloved. He charts this path by using the erotic imagery of the Song of Songs, interpreting the bride as the soul and the bridegroom as Christ, not in his humanity but as Logos or Word. He quotes the first verse of the Song of Songs:

" 'Let him kiss me with the kiss of the mouth,' she said. Now who is this 'she'? The bride. But why bride? Because she is the soul thirsting for God…The one who asks for a kiss, she is a lover." Bernard continues: "Among all the endowments of man, love holds the first place, especially when it is directed to God. No sweeter names can be found to embody that sweet interflow of affections between the Word and the soul, than bridegroom and bride."[116]

Bernard's writings are not exceptional. Much, but not all, of mystical literature is charged with erotic imagery. What does this mean for spirituality and mysticism? Are the fires of spiritual desire disguised sexual energy? Is the ecstasy of mystical union sublimated orgasm? As I will spell out shortly, I believe there is abundant evidence that the intensity of energy the mystics encounter on the divine level far surpasses any biological or sexual energies. This is not to imply that these lesser energies do not contain a spark of the Divine.

Such a complex structure is described by Bonaventure in his treatise *The Soul's Journey into God.* He begins by highlighting the importance of desire in the spiritual journey: "For no one is in any way disposed for divine contemplation that leads to mystical ecstasy unless like Daniel he is *a man of desires* (Dan. 9:23). Such desires are enkindled in us in two ways: by an outcry of prayer that makes us *call aloud in the groaning of our heart* (Ps. 37:9) and by the flash of insight by which the mind turns most directly and intently toward the rays of light."[117] Following a Neoplatonic path, Bonaventure contemplates the rays of divine light shining in the material world, in the soul, and in God himself until in the final stage of the ascent his affectivity passes over completely into the fire of divine love. He speaks in the passionate language of the mystics to evoke in us a glimpse of the intensity of that infinite energy that is the divine life. Bonaventure speaks of "the fire that totally enflames and carries us into God by ecstatic unctions and burning affections. This fire is God and *his furnace is in Jerusalem.*" (Isa. 31:9).[118]

I would like to note here that spiritual writers also treat the rejection of desire in the spiritual life, as well as the journey of the soul beyond the divine light and fire into the desert or emptiness of the Divinity. Although I will not explore the issue now, I believe this polarity can be seen as part of *coincidentia oppositorum*, or the integration of opposites, that permeates the spiritual life.
The Multi-Leveled Psyche

How can we bring together into one coherent model of the psyche such disparate energies as the classical mystics and contemporary psychotherapists describe? I believe that it can be done through the model of the multi-leveled psyche. I will cite such a model in Teresa of Avila and in Jung. In her major mystical work *The Interior Castle,* Teresa of Avila compares the soul to a castle with many rooms and uses the image as a comprehensive model of the psyche and of the spiritual journey. She considers "our soul to be like a castle made entirely out of a diamond or of very clear crystal, in which there are many rooms, just as in heaven there are many dwelling places."[119] She conceives of these rooms or dwelling places arranged on various levels and in various relationships to the center, where the King dwells: "Well, let us consider that this castle has, as I said, many dwelling places: some up above, others down below, others to the side; and in the center and middle is the main dwelling place where the very secret exchanges between God and the soul take place."[120]

The soul or psyche as a dwelling place, a house, a castle, or a temple is an archetypal symbol that occurs both in mystical writings and in contemporary psychotherapy. In the mystical texts the focus is on the Divinity at the center. After moving through the rooms of the house, the levels of the castle, the precincts of the temple, the soul reaches the center—the holy of holies, the marriage chamber—where it is united to the Divinity in ecstatic contemplation or mystical marriage. The movement is from the outer to the inner, from the material to the spiritual, to the Divine. This parallels the ascent symbols, such as the ladder, the mountain, the passage from earth to heaven. Unlike the temple, or dwelling place, these symbols are exterior, symbolizing the various levels of being one traverses in the spiritual journey. Yet their meaning is the same since the spiritual journey is an interior journey.

When we look at the many-leveled psyche in psychotherapy, we do not see the same movement from the material to the Divine. In fact the movement seems to be the reverse, a plunge into the material, the instinctual, the archaic, in order to remove the obstacles, blockages in the flow of libidinal energy. For Freud the goal of the process is the mature personality who is free to work and love—not union with the Divine. It is true that in Jung the process of individuation culminates in the archetype of the Self, which is a symbol of the Divine; nevertheless the goal here, too, is the differentiated and integrated Self, not union with God.

To illustrate this thrust of psychotherapy, I would like to cite the dream that Jung had when he was traveling together with Freud to the United States in 1909. This was a crucial dream in his break with Freud for it led to his theory of the collective unconscious. He tells this dream in *Memories, Dreams, Reflections*:

> This was the dream. I was in a house I did not know, which had two stories. It was "my house." I found myself in the upper story, where there was a kind of salon furnished with fine old pieces in rococo style. On the walls hung a number of precious old paintings. I wondered that this should be my house, and thought, "Not bad." But then it occurred to me that I did not know what the lower floor looked like. Descending the stairs, I reached the ground floor. There everything was much older, and I realized that this part of the house must date from about the fifteenth or sixteenth century. The furnishings were medieval; the floors were of red brick. Everywhere it was rather

dark. I went from one room to another, thinking. "Now I really must explore the whole house." I came upon a heavy door, and opened it. Beyond it, I discovered a stone stairway that led down into the cellar. Descending again, I found myself in a beautifully vaulted room which looked exceedingly ancient. Examining the walls, I discovered layers of brick among the ordinary stone bricks, and chips of brick in the mortar. As soon as I saw this I knew that the walls dated from Roman times. My interest by now was intense. I looked more closely at the floor. It was of stone slabs, and in one of these I discovered a ring. When I pulled it, the stone slab lifted, and again I saw a stairway of narrow stone steps leading down into the depths. These, too, I descended, and entered a low cave cut into the rock. Thick dust lay on the floor, and in the dust were scattered bones and broken pottery, like remains of a primitive culture. I discovered two human skulls, obviously very old and half disintegrated. Then I awoke.[121]

Altered States Research

Where can we find a model of the psyche comprehensive enough to encompass Teresa's interior castle and Jung's dream? Or to put it in more general terms: a model of the psyche to encompass the areas of the psyche explored in spirituality and those explored in psychotherapy. I do not believe that we will find such a model either in classical spiritual writings or in the investigations of twentieth-century psychotherapy. Yet there is such a model at hand. I am referring to the model that has emerged out of the research into altered states of consciousness pursued in the 1960s and 1970s, especially the investigations of the team of Robert Masters and Jean Houston, and later Stanislav Grof. Both the Masters and Houston team and Grof used psychedelic drugs to explore these states of consciousness. After the first phase of their research using drugs, Masters and Houston explored altered states without the use of drugs for some ten years. Through such techniques as hypnosis, sensory deprivation, and sensory overload, they were able to explore the major realms of the psyche as effectively as with psychedelic drugs. It was my privilege to work with them chiefly during this later phase of their research.

The use of this material is problematic from several points of view, but it is so rich and revealing for our present concerns that I believe it should be brought into the discussion. The model of the psyche that emerges out of this research can provide precisely what we need at the present time to investigate the complex relation between spirituality and psychotherapy. I am not proposing that this is the ultimate model of the psyche. In fact, I doubt if humans will ever discover such a model, for the psyche is far too vast and multi-dimensional to be encapsulated in that fashion. It is a model, however, that can throw light on that borderline area where spirituality and psychotherapy contact and interpenetrate each other.

The most important finding from their research is that the psyche has distinct levels, or horizons of consciousness, and that these are linked in complex ways. On the levels of consciousness, Grof and Masters and Houston have similar findings although at times they view them from different perspectives. I will use the formulation of Masters and Houston on the four major levels of consciousness according to the terminology they employed in the earlier phase of their research, since I believe this earlier terminology is more sharply focused than that employed in their book, *The Varieties of Psychedelic Experience.*[122]

The levels that their subjects explored were the following: (1) the *sensorium*, the realm of heightened sense experience; (2) the *ontogenetic* realm, where subjects explored their personal past on a level of deep affect. This realm is comparable, but not limited to, the areas explored in Freudian psychoanalysis; (3) the *phylogenetic* level, where subjects explored the great archetypal symbols, myths, and rituals that are the heritage of the human community as a whole. This is similar to the realm of the collective unconscious of Jung; (4) the level of the *mysterium*, where subjects experience ultimate reality or the highest levels of consciousness. This realm is similar to that experienced by the mystics in the world's religions.

The Sensorium and Ontogenetic Levels

After taking a dosage of a psychedelic drug, subjects usually first experienced heightened sensation in this stage. It was typical for subjects to express wonder at the beauty of ordinary objects. In an example cited by Houston and Masters, the guide handed the subject an orange, which the subject contemplated for several minutes and exclaimed: "Magnificent... I never really saw color before... It's brighter than a thousand suns... (Feels the whole surface of the orange with palms and fingertips)...But this is a pulsing thing...a living pulsing thing....And all these years I've just taken it for granted."[123] These experiences are usually highly aesthetic, often involving complex geometrical forms emerging from the subject's imagination. The following typical testimony of a subject is cited by Grof: "I was deeply enmeshed in an abstract world of whirling geometric forms and exuberant colors that were brighter and more radiant than anything I have ever seen in my life. I was mesmerized by this incredible show."[124] Grof comments that these aesthetic responses on the first level represent the most superficial level of the LSD experience. They do not reveal the subject's unconscious and can be experienced largely as a result of chemical stimulation of the sensory organs.[125]

The situation is quite different on the second, or ontogenetic level. Here the subject enters into his or her past as this is retained in the personal unconscious. The subject explores a world of memories, of persons and events and a tangle of human relations, bringing into consciousness psychodynamic processes, breaking through defenses, unlocking repressed affect. This is the familiar world of psychoanalysis, especially in the tradition of Freud. Masters and Houston give the example of a subject who in an LSD session experienced again his deep emotions at the death of his grandmother when he was not quite four years old. "Suddenly," he said, "I felt as if some obstacle were coming up to me—something large, dark and vague, but very powerful—as if it were knocking on the walls of consciousness… It's Granny's death! I must examine Granny's death!" As a matter of fact, through a year of psychoanalysis the subject had begun to discern that his grandmother's death had been a major traumatic experience in his life, but he was unable to get to the feelings behind it. In the LSD session he was able to break through defenses and feel a surge of guilt experienced years before over his grandmother's death, but which he repressed. He dashed to the bathroom where he went through the movements of vomiting up his identification with his grandmother and the burden of guilt surrounding her death.[126] Speaking of this level of the psyche, Grof observes: "The psychosexual dynamics and the fundamental conflicts of the human psyche as described by Freud are manifested with unusual clarity and vividness in sessions of naive subjects who have never been analyzed."[127]

The Phylogenetic Level

In the research of Masters and Houston, about 40 percent of the subjects entered the third, or phylogenetic, level of the psyche. This is the realm of mythic symbols, of ritual, of Jung's collective unconscious—perhaps the most tantalizing realm of the psyche to account for, since it is not the storehouse of memories from our personal past, but a treasury of symbols that transcend our personal horizons and in some sense are universal. It is striking what powerful psychic energy flows from this level. The subject who makes the passage to this realm feels this concentration of energy in the symbols and rituals, surpassing by far the intensity of even the most traumatic events on the ontogenetic level. It is here, too, that the subject experiences the fundamental creativity of the psyche, for this primordial energy is healing and transforming. There is reason to think the underlying dynamism of this level is the archetype of creative transformation.

These qualities are illustrated in the following case reported by Masters and Houston of a twenty-seven year-old subject, a bookkeeper and a high school graduate whose reading usually was limited to the daily newspaper and popular magazines.

The guide initiated the ritual process by suggesting to the subject that he was attending the rites of Dionysus and was carrying a thyrsus in his hand. When he asked for some details the subject was told only that the thyrsus was a staff wreathed with ivy and vine leaves, terminating at the top in a pine cone, and was carried by the priests and attendants of Dionysus, a god of the ancient Greeks. To this S nodded, sat back in his chair with eyes closed, and then remained silent for several minutes. Then he began to stamp the floor, as if obeying some strange internal rhythm. He next proceeded to describe a phantasmagoria consisting of snakes and ivy, streaming hair, dappled fawn skins, and dances going faster and faster to the shrill high notes of the flute and accelerating drums. The frenzy mounted and culminated in the tearing apart of living animals.

The scene changed and S found himself in a large amphitheater witnessing some figures performing a rite or play. This changed into a scene of white-robed figures moving in the night towards an open cavern. In spite of her intention not to give further clues, the guide found herself asking the subject at this point: " 'Are you at Eleusis?' S seemed to nod 'yes,' whereupon the guide suggested that he go into the great hall and witness the mystery." He responded: "I can't. It is forbidden... I must confess... I must confess..." (The candidate at Eleusis was rejected if he came with sinful hands to seek enlightenment. He must confess, make reparation, and be absolved. Then he received his instruction and then finally had his experience of enlightenment and was allowed to witness the mystery. How it happened that this subject was aware of the stages of the mystery seemed itself to be a mystery). S then began to go the motions of kneading and washing his hands and appeared to be in deep conversation with someone. Later, he told the guide that he had seemed to be standing before a priestly figure and had made a confession. The guide now urged the subject to go into the hall and witness the drama. This he did, and described seeing a "story" performed about a mother who looks the world over for her lost daughter and finally finds her in the world of the underground (the Demeter-Kore story which, in all likelihood, was performed at Eleusis).

This sequence dissolved and the subject spoke of seeing a kaleidoscopic pattern of many rites of the death and resurrection of a god who appeared to be bound up in some way with the processes of nature. S described several of the rites he was viewing, and from his descriptions the guide was able to recognize remarkable similarities to rites of Osiris, Attis, and Adonis. S was uncertain as to whether these rites occurred in rapid succession or all at the same time. The rites disappeared and were replaced by the celebration of the Roman Catholic Mass. Seeking to restore the original setting, the guide again suggested the image of thyrsus. S imagined the thyrsus, but almost immediately it "turned into" a man on a tree (the Christ archetype). The guide then said: "You are thyrsus," to which S responded: "I am thyrsus....I am the thyrsus....I have labored in the vineyard of the world, have suffered, have died, and have been reborn for your sake and shall be exalted forevermore."[128]

Another remarkable experience is recorded by Grof in an LSD session of a clergyman:

> I began to experience the passion of our Lord Jesus Christ. I was Christ, but I was also everyone as Christ and all men died as we made our way in the dirgelike procession toward Golgotha. At this time in my experience there was no longer any confusion; the visions were perfectly clear. The pain was intense, and the story was just, just agonizing. It was at this point that a blood tear from the face of God began to flow, and it began to flow out over the world as God himself participated in the death of all men and in the suffering of all men. The sorrow of this moment is still so intense that it is difficult for me to speak of it. We moved toward Golgotha, and there in agony greater than any I have ever experienced, I was crucified with Christ and all men on the cross. I was Christ, and I was crucified, and I died.[129]
>
> This was followed by a resurrection experience: "When all men died on the cross, there began the most heavenly music I have ever heard in my entire life; it was incredibly beautiful. It was the voice of angels singing, and we began slowly to rise."[130]

The Mysterium Level

Only a small number of subjects of Masters and Houston reached the fourth, or mysterium, level. This realm is radically different from the other three. It is the domain of the Absolute, the Divinity, the Divine Attributes, the Infinite. Here the energy is extreme, unsurpassable. It is energy flowing with unlimited creativity and at the same time suffused with unfathomable peace. The accounts of these subjects reflect those of the great mystics of the world, as is illustrated in the following report:

I, who seemed to have no identity at all, yet experienced myself as *filled with God*, and then as (whatever this may mean) *passing through God and* into a Oneness wherein it seemed God, Being, and a mysterious unnameable One constituted together what I can only designate the ALL. What "I" experienced in this ALL, so far transcends my powers of description that to speak, as I must, of an ineffably rapturous Sweetness is an approximation not less feeble than if I were to describe a candle and so hope to capture with my words all of the blazing glory of the sun.[131]

Interrelation of Levels

I would like to comment on the interrelation of these levels in the light of my ten years of work with Robert Masters and Jean Houston. There is an energy in each of the first three levels that leads to the next—ultimately to the mysterium. This, I believe, constitutes the spiritual journey as an archetype imprinted on the psyche. From each level the subject can break into the mysterium: for example, through the beauty revealed in the sense world on the first level, the subject can break through to the absolute beauty of the mysterium. The ontogenetic level has a strong energy of memory drawing one back into the past in order to heal and release creative energy towards future development and integration. But like Augustine, if the subject goes back far enough through memory into the ground of his or her past, the divine light can manifest itself at the ground of the soul just as it can as the goal of personal growth.

The same is true of the phylogenetic level. The collective memory of the race can draw us back to divine origins and lead us toward the divine fulfillment in the eschaton. There has to be a very strong connection between the phylogenetic level and the mysterium, since the archetype of creative transformation is focused on the transcendence of the realm of the mysterium. It is interesting that often when a problem arises on the ontogenetic level, the psyche will not attempt to solve it there, but rather the subject will be spontaneously drawn into the phylogenetic level where its more powerful energies will provide a solution. The same is true between the phylogenetic and the mysterium levels. A problem, such as the threat of death, on the phylogenetic level may be resolved by the energies emanating from the eternal sphere of the mysterium.

This interlocking of energies shows how organically knit together the levels are. As I have indicated, Freud seems to have explored the ontogenetic level, and Jung the phylogenetic; their approaches serve to heal and release energies that provide resources for the psyche to make the later phase of the journey: into the mysterium. However, one of the problems of contemporary psychotherapy is that it does not have a clear view of the mysterium level. Even Jung, whose archetype of the Self includes the God-image, has not explored this realm. The great spiritual journeys always move here, whether they be described as the highest state of consciousness, as in Buddhism, or as the ontologically absolute, as in the majority of the traditions. This silence on the part of psychotherapy presents problems in trying to explore possible relations between psychotherapy and spirituality. It is here that the psychedelic research can play a mediating role.

Relation of Psychotherapy and Spirituality

The great spiritual teachers in the world's religions chart the stages of the soul's journey towards and into the mysterium, whether this is expressed in levels of being as the Neoplatonic mystics do in Judaism, Islam, and Christianity and the Vedanta mystics do in Hinduism, or exclusively in levels of consciousness as the Buddhists do by bracketing out metaphysics. Whether in terms of being or consciousness, the mystics climb up the ladder of ascent from the material, to the spiritual, to the mysterium. Or they proceed through a procession of purgation, illumination, and union, which is translated in terms of purgation of the material, the illumination of the spiritual, and union with the mysterium—or the achievement of Buddhist enlightenment as mysterium consciousness.

From the standpoint of these spiritual paths, the journeys on the ontogenetic and phylogenetic levels can be seen as preparations and parallel journeys towards the mysterium: by purging obstacles from one's personal past in Freudian analysis, leading through the stages of psychosexual development to full adulthood, and by continuing the journey on the phylogenetic level in Jung's process of individuation, which leads the pilgrim to the threshold of the mysterium. On both levels, the ontogenetic and phylogenetic, the path leads through purgation, illumination, and union—or greater integration of the personality and hence advancement towards the mysterium. Yet this does not tell the whole story. I believe that psychotherapy is more than a preparation for the spiritual journey, more than the handmaiden or servant of spirituality. I believe that it is making a contribution within the realm of spirituality itself, that it is making available a new spirituality of matter. In order to see the full impact of this claim, I invite you to look briefly at an important event in the history of spirituality.

The Axial Period

If we take a broad view of the history of consciousness, we can see that a striking transformation is consciousness occurred in the first millennium BC in three geographical regions: China, India and Persia, and the Eastern Mediterranean, including Israel and Greece. This transformation took place apparently without significant influence of one area upon the other. Karl Jaspers, who first called attention to this phenomenon, calls this the Axial Period, because it "gave birth to everything which since then, man has been able to be." He continues: "It would seem that this axis of history is to be found in the period around 500 BC, in the spiritual process that occurred between 800 and 200 BC. It is there that we meet with the most deep-cut dividing line in history. Man, as we know him today, came into being. For short, we may style this the 'Axial Period.' "[132]

In the Axial Period the transformation of consciousness was mediated by great spiritual teachers who emerged in the three pivotal regions. Confucius and Lao-Tzu appeared in China; the Upanishadic sages, Mahāvira, and the Buddha in India; Zoroaster in Persia[133]; the prophets Elijah, Isaiah, and Jeremiah in Israel; and the philosophers Socrates, Plato, and Aristotle in Greece. These teachers brought about a transformation from the mythic, cosmic, ritualistic, collective consciousness of primal peoples to the rational, analytic, critical, individualistic consciousness that has characterized the mainstream of human history since the Axial Period.

In the Axial Period there emerged a sense of independent, individual identity. No longer was the human person fused with the cosmos and the tribe; rather, persons could separate themselves from the cycles of the seasons and the fertility of nature and embark on their own individual spiritual journey. No longer were persons embedded in the matrix of tribe; rather, they could radically criticize the structure of society, as did Socrates and the Hebrew prophets. No longer were they related to the universe and events through myth and ritual; rather, they would use newly acquired analytic reason to determine the scientific structure of the natural world and record the events of history. With their capacity for abstract reasoning, they created philosophy, analyzing the very structures of being. In fact, they could turn analytic, reflective consciousness inward, arriving at a new awareness of their own capacities and of their place in nature and history.

It was during this period that the world religions as we know them came into existence. Although they have their roots in the pre-Axial Period, their present form embodies the distinctive consciousness of the Axial Period. In fact, their message can be seen as charting of the spiritual path within the horizon of Axial consciousness. This is true of the religions that crystallized in this period: Hinduism, Buddhism, Jainism, Zoroastrianism, Taoism, Confucianism, and Judaism. It is true also of the religions that appeared later but with roots in this period: Christianity, Islam, and Sikhism.

This was a decisive moment in the history of spirituality, for with the emergence of individual identity, the spiritual core of the person came to consciousness. This released enormous spiritual energies drawing the soul into the mysterium. In the great religions of the Axial Period, the individual spiritual path became a possibility. Because of the emergence of individual identity, the person could now come to a self-reflexive grasp of his or her psyche in relation to the Good, according to the Greeks, or of his or her *Atman* in relation to Brahman, according to the Indians. The journey of the inner way could now be pursued, disengaged from cosmic rhythms and rituals and from the collectivity of the tribe. But there was loss as well as gain. Axial spiritual seekers lost their rootedness in the material and biological realms.

I believe that the human community is presently going through a Second Axial Period, which is calling for a rediscovery of our rootedness in matter and the earth. This is seen in the emergence of the feminine, a concern for ecology, and in general a concern for holistic spirituality. It is in this context that we can ultimately understand the relation of psychotherapy and classical spirituality. I believe that psychotherapy is one of the major forces ushering in this new dimension to classical spirituality. But the two must be united as a *coincidentia oppositorum*, an integration of opposites, in a holistic relation that negates neither, but that releases the creativity of both in a new dynamic whole. What I am suggesting is the integration of the two images of the psyche that have come out of psychotherapy and spirituality. Jung's many-leveled house with stairways going down into the caverns of our primordial past and Teresa's image of the soul as a many-faceted Diamond and an Interior Castle with many dwelling places leading ultimately to the Center, where the fires of desire reach their ultimate intensity and peace in the embrace of the mystical marriage in the heart of the mysterium.

Chapter 9
Interreligious Dialogue
and the Future of Hermeneutics

For over a century hermeneutics has been a burning issue in Western thought. In religious circles it has emerged as a challenge to tradition: how to read the Bible in the face of the higher criticism of the nineteenth century, of history, science, psychoanalysis and Marxism? In response to this challenge, theologians have produced form criticism, genre analysis, demythologizing and liberation theology. In political, social and economic circles it has led to a stripping away of the masks of power: of ideology, economic oppression, colonialism, imperialism. In philosophical circles, it has probed radically into the presuppositions of language, symbol, science and human existence itself. In the midst of this ferment, Professor Enrico Castelli has made a unique contribution; for in his yearly conferences at the University of Rome he has drawn together many of the leading thinkers of Europe in an on-going exploration of these complex issues. In an age of fragmentation, he exercised his intellectual acumen and personal charm to produce a collaborative effort among scholars from many nations. In an age of complexity and confusion, his leadership has led to a clarification of issues, a sharp focus on central questions and an on-going creative enquiry. In gratitude for having been part of this process in recent years and as a personal testimony to Professor Castelli, I would like to devote this present article to examine what I discern to be a new phase of the issue of hermeneutics: the emergence of hermeneutics into a global context.

Global Consciousness

From a transnational perspective, the most distinctive event in the last half of the twentieth century is the emergence of global consciousness. After World War II, the forces of technology, industrial expansion and population growth combined to produce a network of communications that brought the peoples of the world into much closer relationship. The eminent historian Jean Leclercq refers to this as a "mutation," a radical change in our historical situation, breaking our continuity with the past and producing a new cultural matrix.[134] Teilhard de Chardin saw this change as a decisive phase in what he called "planetization." Because the earth is a sphere, when world population reached certain stage, peoples can no longer diverge, setting out towards new horizons. Rather they must turn towards each other, entering into more intense interrelations. At an early phase in human evolution the forces of divergence impelled tribes to separate; now, however, in the recent past the forces of convergence have taken the ascendency, drawing peoples into a more complex form of "planetized" consciousness.[135]   For Teilhard, this "planetized" consciousness is not flatly uniform, but contains a rich diversity. It is a complexified form of consciousness in which differentiation is maintained through what he calls "creative unions."

In this age of "mutation"—of "planetization"—the great cultures along with their religious and philosophical heritage are meeting in a new way. The religions are encountering one another in a mood of ecumenism and dialogue, rather than rejection and conflict. Within Christianity the ecumenical spirit, which emerged first among Christian denominations, has now extended itself to world religious. Both the World Council of Churches and the Vatican have established official offices for interreligious dialogue.[136] For over a hundred years research into the history of religions has produced a vast body of knowledge on the diverse phenomena of religions of the world. Sacred texts have been edited and translated; theologies and philosophies have been analyzed and assimilated by the academic community.

What does this mean for hermeneutics? It presents a challenge for Western culture to bring its hermeneutical tradition into this newly forming global context. It is a time for critical assessment and creative development. The religious hermeneutics of the West must ask more radical questions than it did in the face of science, secularization, demythologization—all of which were predominantly Western phenomena. In the encounter with other cultures, other philosophies, other religions, it must ask itself whether it can continue on its present course or whether it, too, must go through a stage of "mutation"— whether hermeneutics itself must be radically transformed by a quantum leap before it can take its place within this new global environment. What is this "mutation", this quantum leap? Western hermeneutics must open itself to pluralism. It must strip itself of its cultural parochialism—its intellectual imperialism—and be willing to accept on its own terms the religious experience of non-Western cultures.

Professor Castelli himself has prepared for this breakthrough in several ways: by drawing the forces of Western hermeneutics into a concerted effort at self-understanding; by articulating in his own writings, and in his formulation of issues for his conference, his sense of radical transcendence in the religious sphere—a transcendence that stands beyond any conceptual formulation of cultural context; and by providing a forum, through his conferences and the publication of their proceedings, for an articulation of cross-cultural hermeneutics. From the very first meeting of the conference in 1961, this cross-cultural perspective has been present, chiefly through the contribution of Raimundo Panikkar. These contributions through the years have issued in the recent publications by Panikkar of a major book on cross-cultural hermeneutics entitled Myth, Faith and Hermeneutics.[137] The larger portion of this book is drawn from some ten papers which Panikkar presented in the sessions of the Castelli conference, from 1961 to 1974.

In the present paper I would like to explore the transformation of Western hermeneutics required for it to move into a global environment. In doing this, I will draw upon certain themes which I have developed in papers for the Castelli conferences from 1973 through 1978.[138] As in these papers, I will reflect the pluralistic mood of the United States, viewing it in relation to a pluralistic global culture. I will examine: 1) the need for Western hermeneutics to open itself to the varieties of depth religious experience of other cultures; 2) the corres-ponding need to pluralize hermeneutics by allowing it to emerge out of these varieties of religious experience; 3) the nature of the pluralistic unity that can be maintained in a global community. The reader can observe that this is a Trinitarian perspective, in that the depth religious experience reflects the Father as source, the hermeneutical interpretation reflects the Son as his image, and the unity in diversity reflects the Holy Spirit. This Trinitarian perspective has been present both implicitly and explicitly in my previous papers. In using the Trinity, I may seem to go counter to the very openness to other religions that I have previously espoused. As will become clear as I proceed, this Trinitarian perspective merely reflects the fact that I come out of a Christian theological background. By employing this Trinitarian perspective self-consciously, I can be aided by its value and at the same time restrained from imposing it on those who are not Christian.

The Varieties of Religious Experience

The first phase of transforming hermeneutics consists of opening ourselves to the varieties of religious experience, especially those of a culture and religion other than our own. A wealth of data can be gleaned from the history of religious as well as from studies in the psychology of religious experience in the tradition of William James's The Varieties of Religious Experience.[139] We must be open not only to variety but also, and especially, to depth. It is crucial that we plunge to the level of depth religious experience as our point of departure for hermeneutics. If we are interpreting religious texts, we must not remain on the verbal—or conceptual—level, but must go beyond these to the primordial religious experience they are expressing. We must ask: What is the experience behind a text of the Koran, a Hindu sutra, a mystic's prayer? And we must ask not merely about the surface of that experience, but its very depths. What is the primordial religious experience expressed in these texts? What is its structure? Its dynamics? To reach this experience and to clarify it, we must employ a foundational phenomenology of religious consciousness. Such a phenomenology may discover patterns of unity in the varieties of primordial religious experience, and it may even arrive at an underlying unity behind all the diversity. At this point I am prescinding from that possibility and focusing on the diversity itself since it is precisely this that must be recognized at the present stage in the movement towards global consciousness.

Although both the history of religions and the psychology of religion offer resources for the trans-formation of hermeneutics, even more important is the dialogue of world religions. For the dialogue of religions is a living encounter. It is a meeting of person with person, believer with believer – and more significantly, of living faith with living faith, of religious experience with religious experience. In this encounter, on does not bracket his own faith; he grounds himself in his faith and opens his consciousness to the faith of the other. Such a meeting—and its consequent dialogue—requires a complex form of religious consciousness on the part of all the participants. They must not be mere objective observers of each other. Grounded in his faith and open to the other, each must perceive the religious experience of the other as authentic and as a value—not only for the other but for himself. The Christian must empathize with the Buddhist's experience, and the Buddhist with the Christian's—not merely in its common dimensions, but in its very diversity; and each must accept this diverse experience as a religious value in itself and as an enrichment of one's own religious reality. When traditions are similar, the participants must beware of failing to be sensitive to differences. For example, the Christian must empathize with the Muslim's awareness of the transcendence of God, but not in the Christian modality, in which the divine transcendence is mediated through Christ—but precisely as the Muslim experiences transcendence, without the mediational experience which is at the center of Christianity.

In the West the openness to experience and to pluralism is characteristic of the United States. Its own political past has attempted to deal with the pluralism caused by the many waves of immigration of diverse peoples. More recently the United States has been the center of a new wave of what might be called spiritual immigration. Missionaries from Hinduism, Buddhism and

Sufism have brought their spiritual techniques to a generation of youth who felt alienated from their cultural past. In the late sixties and early seventies this produced what can be called an "experience explosion."[140] Although this ferment reflects in a distinctly American way the larger and more complex pluralism of the emerging global environment, it runs the risk of being superficial, of dissipating its energies, of merely evoking a conservative reaction rather than a creative development. Furthermore, because of its empirical cast of mind, America has not cultivated the type of self-reflective critical consciousness that is characteristic of European intellectual culture. It was this European intellectual tradition—with its emphasis on self-reflective logos—that produced the science of hermeneutics. It may well be that the strategic way to draw Western religious consciousness into a global context is to produce a happy marriage between the American openness to varieties of religious experience and European self-reflective logos. Such a marriage would require concessions on both sides: American experience would have to become more self-reflective; European logos would have to become more grounded in experience and at the same time pluralized by the very diversity of experience. We now turn to the logos side of this proposed marriage, viewing its relation to the pluralistic type of depth religious experience we have just examined.

Hermeneutics and the Logos of Experience

In our present perspective, hermeneutics is not merely the science of the interpretation of a text, but the science of the interpretation of experience. This text is crucial, of course, but only as an expression of experience. The history of religions, if it is heavily based on textual studies, runs the risk of analyzing only the logos of the text itself and not its underlying experience. The dialogue of religions, on the other hand, brings us into immediate contact with the experience; for the dialogue takes place within the experiential environment. The dialogue involves logos; for it is, as its etymology suggests, a dia-logos, a word, an expression, a communication, an exchange, which contains intelligible form and rhetorical expression, but which emerges out of primordial religious experience, reflects the intelligible form of that experience to the believer and images it to the other with whom he speaks.

At this point we can be assisted by considering the Trinity, especially by seeing the human person as an image of the Trinity.[141] The relation between experience and expression reflects the relation between the Father and the Son in the Christian understanding of the Trinity. Primordial depth religious experience would correspond to the Father in the Trinity as the fountain source of the divinity, the divine depth which expresses itself in its consubstantial

Image and Word, who is called its very offspring or Son. The Father, then, is the abyss of the divinity, the divine silence—but he is also that primordial divine energy which breaks the eternal silence with an eternal Word. Between the Father and the Son there is perfect equality but not identity: for the Son is the perfect Image of the Father, but he is not the Father. In the case of the human person, the logos level is not identical with the experiential level; yet it expresses the experience. The experience is not without logos, but it is not identical with logos. It contains logos, and yet it transcends logos. In the Trinity there is only one Logos, who is the perfect Image of the Father; in the human person there must be many logoi, for unlike the Father in the Trinity, the human person cannot image himself perfectly; nor does he at any moment reflect the unfathomable depth of the Father. The fact that he is only a partial image of the Trinity accounts for the fact that there are in human history many primordial religious experiences since there are many ways in which humans participate in that divine abyss. Hence there are diverse images, concepts, words expressing that primordial abyss.

Each primordial experience—reflecting an aspect of that abyss—has its own distinctive logos. This is crucial for cross-cultural, interreligious hermeneutics. In the dialogue of religions, one must not assume the logos of the other is identical with his own, or that it is expressing the same aspect of the abyss. The Christian must ask himself whether the logoi of the Buddhist, the Hindu, the Muslim are expressing different primordial experiences from his own. He must also ask himself whether it is possible to translate between his Christian logos and the logoi of the others in the dialogue. Although I believe that some translation is possible, the proper hermeneutical method would be to let the logos lead one back to that primordial experience of the abyss which it is expressing. This is a method similar to what the medieval Christian theologians called reductio, etymologically a leading back, and in theology a leading back to a source.[142] Since logos has sprung from this source, to interpret the logos, one must be led back through the logos to primordial wellspring from which it has issued. The Christian must lead the Hindu's logoi back to the latter's primordial experience and then discern how the Hindu's logoi express that experience in its uniqueness.

I am suggesting here that there is no universal expression, no universal language, no universal conceptual scheme, which expresses univocally all the varieties of primordial religious experience. Hence there is no universal hermeneutics, if hermeneutic is taken as a logos content; I am, however, proposing this reductio of logoi to experience as a universal method of interpretation. Religious hermeneutics, then, would be defined as the science that guides the process of reductio of logos to primordial experience.[143] It is extremely important that the Christian does not interpret the Buddhist texts by reducing the Buddhist logos to his Christian primordial experience. The same is true, of course, for the Buddhist in relation to the Christian. Such an awareness on the part of the participants in the dialogue acknowledges the pluralism of both logos and primordial experience and allows hermeneutics to operate scientifically in a cross-cultural context.

The Global Spirit: Unity in Diversity

This leads us to the third element in the Trinity: the Holy Spirit. In the Trinity the Spirit is the union of the Father and the Son, the love which binds them together and which overflows into the world. In cosmic terms, the Spirit has been associated with the World Soul, but not identical with it since the Spirit is a transcendent principle, but acting immanently in the world, producing an underlying unity among the diversity of forms in creation. On the level of the human community, the Spirit binds together the Church, inspiring diverse charisms at the same time that it unifies believers in a single divine life. Against this background, we can see a reflection of the Spirit in the emergence of a global community; for the diverse traditions of the world—with their varieties of primordial religious experience and their corresponding logoi—would be moving towards a global unity which does not destroy diversity, but maintains it by a creative interrelation of primordial experience to primordial experience and logoi to logoi.

What form will consciousness take in this global community of the Spirit? What role will hermeneutics play in this new environment? Consciousness will be complexified; and an enlightened hermeneutics will be the vehicle of maintaining unity and diversity. The unity will be a unity of shared primordial religious experience and a unity in the life of the Spirit—not a unity through a specific logos. This is the greatest challenge to Western thought and to its understanding of hermeneutics. For Western culture is preeminently a culture of logos. The West has developed conceptualization, logic and formal analysis, applying these pragmatically to all spheres of life: science, politics, economics and to religion itself. Whatever the limits of logos in other spheres, even the West has been aware of its limits in the sphere of religion; but it has not adequately recognized the diversity of primordial experience we have explored above. For the West to enter into this new complexified consciousness, it must free its own logos from its primordial base and allow it to become pluralized in a new life of the Spirit. The West must realize that such a life in the Spirit is not a denial of Logos, but its further affirmation. To free logos, to pluralize it is not to abandon it, but rather to enrich it; not to make it alogos but to render it even more fully logos: more scientific, more rational.

Already many people in many different quarters are manifesting the multi-dimensional religious consciousness of this global environment. They appear in the dialogue of religions. It is striking that at this moment there are two mentalities sharply etched among those in the dialogue. Some, still echoing the past, relate to other religions only from their own faith and their own conceptual schemes. Others—and they are increasing in number—manifest the complex consciousness described above. They empathize on the experiential level and feel enriched by the faith of the other. This mutual enrichment is the very bond of the life of the Spirit. Out of this bonding comes the new and broader self-reflective logos that requires a pluralized hermeneutics. Another group, not formally involved in interreligious dialogue, discovers this complex consciousness in their own personal spiritual quest. Increasing numbers of persons leave temporarily their Jewish or Christian faith, seeking in the Orient a new spiritual path. Enriched by the spiritual wisdom of the East, many are now returning to their own heritage, without abandoning the spiritual nourishment they received from Buddhism or Hinduism.

Many questions remain. What of the absolute claims of each religion? These cannot be ignored by hiding them under the table, as it were, in order to assure polite acceptance and gentlemanly conversation. Nor can they be camouflaged by a superficial universalism in which mere abstractions attempt to establish relationships that cannot be sustained in life. Absolute claims are part of the very content of interreligious dialogue. The challenge to hermeneutics is to explore whether in this new life of the Spirit, diverse absolute claims can find larger horizons in which they can be maintained without destroying a genuine mutual relation on the level of primordial religious experience.

Practical questions also surface. How to enter pragmatically into this new environment? Previously I have given primacy to the interreligious dialogue over the academic study of religion. From our Trinitarian perspective, the reason for this is now more apparent. Important though the academic study of religion is, it can be merely an exercise in the level of logos, even of limited logos. Dialogue, on the other hand, draws us into the life of the Spirit, since it opens us to community. This sharing in community can stimulate the total

Trinitarian process we have been studying, along with its self-reflective hermeneutics. Out of the shared life of dialogue, the diversity of logos can appear, and manifest the corresponding diversity of primordial religious experience.

One of the greatest obstacles for the West to enter fully into this process is its epistemology. Over the last several centuries, Western philosophy has been entrapped in an epistemology that focuses on individual subjectivity even to the point of solipsism. With such an epistemology, dialogue may be impossible or limited merely to an interpersonal encounter without a genuine sharing of faith. Authentic interreligious dialogue call for Westerners to rediscover what I have called elsewhere their "shamanistic faculty."[144] In primitive religions, the shaman is said to be able to leave his body, fly in spirit to distant places, acquire new knowledge there and return to his body to share this knowledge with others. I believe that we all have a "shamanistic faculty", that is the ability, in the community of dialogue, to leave our own culture and religion and fly into the cultural religious world of the other, experiencing by empathy, its center from within. Then we return, enriched, into our own world to share our new knowledge with those of our own tradition who have not made such a journey. To develop a "shamanistic epistemology", with all of its philosophical implication, is, I believe, one of the most basic tasks of hermeneutics.

In addition to these theoretical and practical questions, larger issues emerge. In the new "planetized" consciousness, will one culture, one religion, one philosophy prevail? Or will a truly pluralized global culture be born? Whatever answer to these questions will be given by the future, this much seems clear at the present: these questions should be raised and pursued in a dialogic context and with a liberated, pluralized hermeneutic.

Chapter 10
My Journey Into Interreligious Dialogue
with Janet Cousins

The Lakota Reservation in South Dakota

My journey into interreligious dialogue began more than forty years ago on a Lakota or Sioux reservation in South Dakota. At that time I was studying theology at a Jesuit seminary in Kansas and could volunteer to spend the summer working with the Brulé Lakota on the Rosebud Reservation. Along with four other seminarians, I worked as an amateur cowboy branding cattle, and also painting window frames, doing handy work in the buildings and on the grounds.

In the evening after work, I would often saddle up a horse and ride into the canyons to visit Chief Hollow Horn Bear, the last official chief of the Brulé Lakota. When I asked him to describe the traditional Lakota religion, he told me the story of the White Buffalo Woman, a heavenly figure, who miraculously appeared to two Lakota braves on the plains. She prophesied that an animal that they had never seen before would come to their village.

If the Lakota welcomed and honored it, then the animal would greatly enhance their lives. This was reported to the tribe who waited in expectation. A short while later a herd of buffalo ran through their village.

When the dust had settled and the buffalo had departed, the Lakota discovered a strange animal that did not resemble a buffalo, rather it looked like a large dog, so they named it "chunckaka" or "big dog." To this day, the Lakota call it "big dog." This animal was the horse! Soon other horses came, and with them the Lakota became the most powerful tribe throughout the plains. On the "winter count," an annual chronology of tribal events, the first time the horse appears is the year Coronado crossed the plains and brought with him horses from Spain. As the White Buffalo Woman had foretold, the gift of the horse enormously enriched the future of the Lakota nation.

On other occasions, I would meet with Jake Kills in Sight, whose grandfather fought with Chief Crazy Horse against General Custer and the Seventh Cavalry. When Custer encountered a huge encampment of Lakota along the Little Big Horn River, he had to flee with his cavalry, but eventually was forced to take a stand. Crazy Horse and his warriors surrounded Custer and his men. Kills in Sight tells the rest of the story. Crazy Horse held his warriors at bay out of firing range. Then he dismounted and picked herbs from the ground and placed them in his war shirt. He then rode directly into Custer's soldiers who fired their rifles directly at Crazy Horse. The bullets hit him in the chest but did not penetrate. They merely fell to the ground. Crazy Horse returned to his warriors and showed them how the bullets left him unscathed. He said to them, "My medicine is strong today!" Then he shouted the Lakota battle cry, "Hoka Hey" or "Welcome, you!" and charged!

Lakota history was very present in the memory of the tribe as I learned from Chief Hollow Horn Bear and Jake Kills in Sight. This was highlighted by the fact that the last survivor of the battle of the Little Big Horn had died only two years before I went to the reservation and the last survivor of the Wounded Knee massacre was still alive and residing not far from the Jesuit mission where I was working.

In this atmosphere, I found myself penetrating deeper and deeper into Lakota culture, their dramatic history and their profound spirituality. I vividly remember the day, while I was talking to a group of Lakota, that I felt my consciousness, as it were, extend itself out of my body and pass over into their consciousness. From that moment I felt I could see things from their perspective and experience their values from within their world. Also I could look back at my own world and see its values in a clearer light—but also its limitations! The insight of the moment grew over the following weeks. I became increasingly aware of human values that the Indians preserved and that we had lost: their love of the land, their organic harmony with nature, their strong tribal ties, their sense of time as a flowing process rather than a static continuum to be divided into endless schedules, their immersion in myth and ritual, whose language and dynamics they understood with a primordial wisdom. I perceived also their religious sensibility: their awareness of the presence of Wakan Tanka, or God, in nature and in their lives. Nature as a whole was sacred to them, as was life in all its dimensions. Certain areas, for example the Black Hills, were especially sacred to the Lakota. Through the sacred ritual of the Sun Dance, they participated in the animal world—especially the buffalo—the tribe and Wakan Tanka.

This experience was decisive for me. It broke the invisible blinders of my own culture and opened an experiential world I had not even dreamed existed. For a while it alienated me from my culture, for I realized that I had been trapped within my culture without knowing it. I became aware that, while my culture had given me values that the Indians had not received, it also deprived me of values that were theirs. Only some five years later was I able to resolve this tension, by traveling to Greece and perceiving how the self-reflective consciousness of Greek culture had emerged out of primal consciousness.

It was decisive academically as well. Since I had discovered a new world of experience through the Indians, I realized that there existed many other such worlds beyond the horizons of my culture that I could explore in many ways.

Some years later, I became aware of a formula that summed up my experiences with the Lakota and with my continued journey into interreligious dialogue. In his book *The Way of All the Earth*, John Dunne[145] of Notre Dame University, describes this process. He writes in his preface: "Is a religion coming to birth in our time? It could be. What seems to be occurring is a phenomenon we might call "passing over," passing over from one culture to another, from one way of life to another, from one religion to another. Passing over is a shifting of standpoint, a going over to the standpoint of another culture, another way of life, another religion." According to Dunne, passing over leads to a return: "it is followed by an equal and opposite process we might call "coming back," coming back with new insight to one's own culture, one's own way of life, one's own religion." Dunne sees this process as characteristic of our time: "Passing over and coming back, it seems is the spiritual adventure of our time." I believe that statement captures the essence of my experience with the Lakota and my continued involvement in interreligious dialogue.

Although I did not have the clarity of John Dunne's formulation, I grasped the essence of dialogic consciousness. Before leaving the Lakota reservation that summer I made a plan to follow with other cultures and religions the same path I had discovered with the Lakota: namely, (1) to immerse myself in the total concrete life world of some followers of a religion; (2) with the plan to participate empathetically in that consciousness; (3) to return enriched to my own. The rest of my life has been a spiritual journey into interreligious dialogue. Where this will ultimately lead it is too early to tell, but for many who have been drawn this way, passing over and coming back is the distinctive spiritual journey of our time.

From South Dakota to Jerusalem

From South Dakota I returned to Kansas to complete my theological studies. However, I was not ordained since for a number of years I discerned that the priesthood was not my vocation. I went to Fordham University for further studies and began a teaching career there that lasted forty years. My arrival in New York coincided with the coming of spiritual teachers from the East: Swami Satchitananda from India, Eido Shimano Roshi from Japan, Brother David Steindl-Rast of Mt. Saviour Monastery, Elmira, New York, and

Rabbi Joseph Gelberman of New York City. During this period I came to know them very well and took part in their programs. In 1968 I participated with them in a conference entitled "EastWest: One Heart" at Princeton Theological Seminary.

At the same time, I had become acquainted with Raimon Panikkar and had been very enriched by his teaching on the Trinity and world religions. Since the ecumenical institute called Tantur was just being established in Jerusalem at that time, he suggested that my family and I spend the academic year there in 1972-1973. This provided me with an extraordinary opportunity to take forward what I had learned about interreligious dialogue with the Lakota Indians in South Dakota.

During the academic year 1972-1973, then, I had the privilege of living, along with my family, in the Ecumenical Institute for Advanced Theological Studies in Jerusalem. This Institute developed out of an initiative proposed by the Protestant observers at the Second Vatican Council to carry on the ecumenical spirit fostered at the Council and to channel it creatively into Christian theology. Living and working together that year were some thirty theologians, representing a wide spectrum of Christian traditions among which were Eastern Orthodox (Greek, Polish, and Rumanian), Roman Catholic, Anglican, Lutheran, Presbyterian, Reformed (Dutch, Belgian, and Swiss), and Seventh Day Adventist. We were privileged to have in our community such leaders in ecumenism as Oscar Culmann and the distinguished Dominican Yves Congar. Living with us at the Institute was also the eminent Old Testament scholar James Sanders who had been assigned the task of editing the Psalms from the Dead Sea scrolls.

Our institute was at a remarkably beautiful site at the city limits of Jerusalem, looking down on Bethlehem and beyond into the Judean Desert. There was a spot on our Institute grounds where we could look down across the desert and the tomb of Herod and see the sun shining like gold on the waters of the Dead Sea. The sights and sounds we experienced every day, for example, of camels and spices, were as exotic to us Americans and Europeans as they were to the Crusaders in the Middle Ages. It was in this setting that I was drawn to "pass over" into the world of Islam as I had previously done with the Lakota in South Dakota.

Since I had been living and teaching in New York City, I had significant contact with Judaism over several years, but very little contact with Islam. In Israel I had abundant opportunities to get to know the Jewish community, to get to know Jewish scholars and to observe the religious practices of the Jewish community. As a result, my main concern was to explore first hand the religious world of Islam. One of my research projects for the Ecumenical Institute consisted in "passing over" into the religious world of Islam, using the techniques I had learned among the Indians: in this case, to share in the everyday life of the Muslims by living in a village and praying with them in mosques.

After some unsuccessful attempts to make contacts, I met a young Muslim named Abdul Jaleel, who invited me to spend time with his family in their tiny village in the mountains outside Hebron. For some five months he took me to mosques in Jerusalem, Bethlehem, Hebron, Gaza, and small villages to pray with Muslims in mosques.

My "passing over" followed the same route as with the Indians. I first became immersed in the everyday world of Arabic culture in the Middle East. As with the Indians, I felt that I passed over into the value experience of that world and could look back both critically and sympathetically on my own world in a new light. I remember very sharply the day on which I passed over into the religious experience of Islam. It was less than two weeks since I had met Abdul Jaleel. After spending the night at our apartment at Tantur, he invited me to attend the Friday service at the great mosque in Bethlehem. Since Friday is the Muslim holy day, the service was longer than usual and attracted a large number of Muslims. Over the period of an hour, I joined in the prayers with several hundred men and listened to the chanting of the Koran by a blind sheik. The intensity of the prayer mounted as the group bowed down repeatedly, touching their heads to the ground in submission to Allah the all-powerful. At the peak of that intensity, I felt that I passed over into the heart of their religious experience. I shared with them their sense of the transcendence of God—of his power and majesty which calls forth a response of worship, so dramatically expressed in the Muslim's bowing to the ground.

This experience of God's transcendence is central to Islam. It is what we, in passing over, must contact as the primary element of the Islamic religious consciousness. Our method must be that of passing over rather than mere analogy to the Christian experience of God's transcendence. We must be cautious not to see Islam as a truncated Christianity or assume that God's transcendence is identical in both Islam and Christianity. In the latter God's transcendence is bound up with his immanence in the Incarnation, a distinct form of immanence which Islam strongly rejects. It is very difficult for Christians to disengage the Incarnational dimension from their religious consciousness. Only by passing over into Islam as a total structure of consciousness, can Christians understand the meaning of such images as being a slave of Allah and of submission to the will of Allah. If we penetrate deeply enough into the experience of Islam, we will discover the positive—even liberating—meaning these images have for Muslims, in spite of the fact that within the structures of Christian consciousness, with its images of freedom, they would seem repressive.

Having passed over into the central experience of Islam, Christians can come back to their own religion enriched with values perceived in Islam. If, like Muslims, they can grasp the value of God's pure transcendence, they might be liberated from some of the negative aspects of their own belief in God's transcendence. Since Christianity focuses so centrally on God's immanence in the Incarnation, transcendence may become a problem for Christians. They might so emphasize God's intimate loving presence in the human sphere in Jesus of Nazareth that they ignore or reject the dimension of transcendence that Christians share with Islam. Transcendence may appear only in a negative light, as God's detached distance from the world or his overwhelming power which threatens the creature's autonomy. By grasping the value of God's transcendence in Islam—unrelated to the Incarnation—Christians can discover a dimension of their own tradition that might otherwise be submerged or rejected.

Thus passing over and coming back yields not only new knowledge of other religions, but a clearer understanding of one's own religion and its complex relationships to other religions.

Conference at the United Nations: October 24, 1975

My journey into interreligious dialogue took a dramatic turn in 1975. In early January I received a telephone call from my friend Jean Houston inviting me to join a committee of the Temple of Understanding that was organizing a conference of world religious leaders to be held in October 1975 at the United Nations. Founded in 1960 by Juliet Hollister, the Temple of Understanding had emerged as a major force for creating understanding and communication among the world's religions. It had assembled an impressive international committee which included, for example, the Dalai Lama. The Temple had organized four major conferences, one of which took place in Calcutta in 1968. It was at this conference that Thomas Merton made his now famous statement: "My dear Brothers and Sisters, we are already one, but we imagine we are not. What we have to recover is our original unity: What we have to be is what we already are."

Merton's statement provided the theme of the UN Conference in 1975: "One Is the Human Spirit." Since the United Nations is built on a secular model, it lacks a structure for bringing religious and spiritual resources into the workings of the UN. It was to fill this gap that the Temple of Understanding proposed such a conference. And it was in this context that I joined the planning committee of the Temple of Understanding in 1975.

This began one of the most remarkable years of my life. For ten months, while I continued to teach my classes at Fordham and Columbia, I was caught up in the world of international diplomacy—a world that shifted every day according to the dynamics of the world community. The Temple's project became part of this world.

Our planning committee of some five members met in January of 1975 at the United Nations headquarters in Manhattan for a meeting with C. V. Narasimhan, then Office Director for Secretary General Kurt Waldheim. The committee agreed to make a proposal that the United Nations host a meeting of world religious leaders at the United Nations. This proposal was directed to the Secretary General, who was already in Vienna en route to a formal visit with the Pope. Within a short time the project was launched. With the aid of Monsignor di Filippo, of the Vatican Observer's office to the UN, I drafted a short letter to Kurt Waldheim, informing him of this initiative and suggesting to him that he bring it to the attention of the Pope. Shortly after that the Austrian attaché came to the office, picked up the letter and placed it in his official mail pouch to be delivered in Vienna the next morning. And so the project was launched.

After a week, word trickled down from the Secretary General's office that Kurt Waldheim had not passed our initiative to the Pope, but to Monsignor Benelli, who was in charge of internal Church affairs. The Monsignor responded to the Secretary General that this was a laudatory project but he was afraid that it would show more the disunity of religions than their unity. As a result the initiative did not move forward.

In this period, I was assigned to report to André Lewin, the spokesman of the Secretary General and attaché for special projects. Once a week I would go to his office at the UN and bring him up to date on the progress of our committee and receive his advice for further development. Of particular concern was the choice of speakers for the final day of the program at the United Nations: one speaker each for Hinduism, Buddhism, Judaism, Christianity, and Islam.

An idea emerged that I should be sent on a mission to take up the idea again and gather support for this initiative with the Christian leadership of Europe and specifically the Vatican. At that time I was officially a consultant to the Vatican Council for interreligious matters and had access to the Vatican. André Lewin, the spokesman to the Secretary General, discussed the matter with Kurt Waldheim, who said he would support the project if we could get the endorsement and official support of the project from the Christian world leaders. So I was sent on an official mission to the Vatican, the World Council of Churches, and the Archbishop of Canterbury. At a meeting of high Vatican officials, Cardinal Pignedoli gave his wholehearted approval of the initiative. At the World Council of Churches in Geneva, I was cordially received by the General Secretary, who said that he could not speak at the UN as a representative of Protestantism since according to the statutes, the World Council was not a representative body. I met the Archbishop of Canterbury at a public event in London, but did not have time to propose the project. Fortunately, the strong support of the Vatican was sufficient to place the plan once again in operation.

Not long after I returned from Europe, I was called to a meeting of those UN officials connected with General Assembly Affairs. The question was where and how could our proposed meeting take place? If a vote of the General Assembly were to take place, the Soviet Union and China would veto it. However, the meeting could be held in the large conference room number four, but not as an official UN event. Eventually, this was also rejected. The event took place in the Dag Hammarskjold Auditorium, which seated three hundred. As the summer and fall approached, some obstacles to the project emerged, but they passed and the project moved into its realization in October as a "Spiritual Summit Conference" and as a landmark event. This was the fifth spiritual summit organized by the Temple of Understanding; others had taken place in Calcutta, Geneva, Princeton Theological Seminary, and Cornell University. This week-long interfaith festival marked the 30th anniversary of the founding of the United Nations. For the first time the world's religious leaders would meet at the United Nations. The actual program had two parts: five days at the Cathedral of St. John the Divine with hundreds of participants and thousands in the audience, and a final day with representative delegates at the United Nations.

The program at the UN had been planned meticulously for more than nine months. The choice of speakers was a matter of paramount concern. After getting adjusted to the ways of the UN, I continued to meet weekly with André Lewin, the spokesman for Secretary General Kurt Waldheim. What he and I discussed was our choice of speakers and their appropriateness for the UN. He was very open to possibilities, but at the same time sensitive to political implications. The choice was not particularly difficult. What was difficult was exploring whether it would be possible to have speakers for Chinese religion: Taoism and Confucianism. The times were particularly problematic. Maoist China was not inclined to look positively on speakers reflecting the classical traditions of China. We tried looking outside mainline China, but this did not prove likely. Eventually, we regretfully gave up.

On the day the conference began, when hundreds of people were milling around St. John the Divine Cathedral, someone came to me and said, "There's a group of about thirty Indians here who want to talk to you." So I met with them in the parish building. When they identified themselves, I realized that we had the top American Indian leadership in the United States, both spiritually and politically. I was thrilled with this but perplexed with how to provide food and lodging and integrate them into the dynamism of the conference. Over the next day I heard reports that some of the Indians were unhappy at how things were developing for them. Just at that moment I saw the Iroquois entering the cathedral with their leaders Mad Bear and Beman Logan. At the same time, Toshio Myake, the head of the international committee of the Temple of Understanding, was arriving. I suggested that we go into the crypt of the cathedral. There we had a "pow-wow" for over two hours. Tensions were resolved and the two Iroquois leaders brought peace among the Native Americans, who made a distinctive contribution to the entire program.

The program opened on Sunday evening with a grand spectacle: a procession of groups of participants, each dressed in their traditional attire: Native Americans arrayed in eagle feathers, Buddhists in saffron robes, and Shinto in their white gowns proceeded down the aisle and around the cathedral. In the opening keynote address in the cathedral, Margaret Mead, the well-known anthropologist, asserted that "at the heart of each religion we find the same overriding concern for our common humanity." All of humankind, she cautioned, faces a common threat to our existence in pollution and advanced weapons. But this common threat brings "new hope," she claimed, because we now share the same concerns. Dr. Mead's concerns would be later shared by the Native Americans at the conference.

The days and evenings were filled with music, chanting, drama, liturgies, and formal discussion. A typical day began with a fire ceremony by the Native Americans in the center of the nave of the cathedral. This was followed by a panel discussion as exemplified by the following: a panel on the "unity of the human community" which was moderated by Xenon Rossides, permanent ambassador of Cyprus to the United Nations. Among the panelists were Princess Poon Diskul, president of the World Fellowship of Buddhists, Muhammed Zafrulla Khan, a Muslim and former president of the United Nations General Assembly; Master Chitrabhanu, a Jain spiritual leader; Dom Leclerq, the leading scholar of Christian monasticism, and Robert Muller, then an official of the United Nations Office for Inter-Agency Affairs and later an Under Secretary General. As the *New York Times* reported this panel: "Observing that there had been 'drastic changes in human and international relations in a world grown utterly interdependent' in the last 30 years, Mr. Rossides said the conference was helping to bring 'the human spirit into the labors of the United Nations.'" Master Chitrabhanu spoke on Jainism's emphasis on reverence for life, but he stressed: 'We don't want to make one religion in the world. You cannot expect a garden of only one flower.'" He has a beautiful capacity to respect and express our religious diversity while recognizing our unity.

At noon each day there was a liturgical event such as a Buddhist or Christian ritual. One of the most elegant was the Shinto ritual performed by almost one hundred who were flown in from Japan especially for this event. Dressed as they were in their white robes, they performed their ritual with consummate grace. In the afternoon groups of ten met in the small chapels surrounding the main altar. At the end of their discussions, group leaders gathered the results for a joint statement to be read at our final session at the United Nations.

In the evening after dinner there were artistic and musical events: on one evening a live symphony orchestra played a composition that was commissioned for the occasion. Another evening we were inspired by a tableau entitled "A Mass On the World," conceived by Pir Vilayat Khan and enacted by a large group of his followers from the Sufi Order of the West. On Thursday evening the participants were treated to a banquet in the Grand Ballroom of the Waldorf Astoria, during which we were entertained by the music of Ravi Shankar. The next day we gathered for the final session in the Dag Hammarskjold auditorium on the premises of the United Nations.

The final meeting at the United Nations featured eminent spiritual leaders, each representing a major religious tradition. Among them were the Buddhist Lord Abbott Kosho Ohtani, the Muslim scholar Seyyed Hossein Nasr, and for Christianity, Mother Teresa, who later would be recognized by a Nobel Peace Prize for her work with the poor and dying on the crowded streets of Calcutta. In a speech which moved her audience to tears, Mother Teresa spoke of the love and dignity given by the Missionaries of Charity to those whom others had deemed too hopeless to care for. She urged the representative group of Hindus, Buddhists, Jews, Christians and Muslims to remember the poor as "brothers and sisters in the same family, created by the same loving God." In one of her stories of the poor she recalled a man who had lived in the gutter and had been brought to the home for the dying. "He said he'd lived like an animal, but would die like an angel with love and care."

The summit ended with a joint statement which called for a "'new spirituality' free of insularity, a plea for religious freedom and a proposal that the United Nations create an agency to bring spiritual resources to bear on world problems." The joint statement affirmed the following:

The horrors of current and possible wars, the destruction of the earth through the abuses of technology, and the vastness of problems confronting the human condition require the rededication of all peoples, in an awakened sense of the unity of the human spirit, to enhance co-operation toward the building of a peaceful and just world.

The crises of our time are challenging the world religions to release a new spiritual force transcending religious, cultural, and national boundaries into a new consciousness of the oneness of the human community and so putting into effect a spiritual dynamic toward the solutions of world problems. . . We affirm a new spirituality, divested of insularity and directed toward a planetary consciousness. . .

In conclusion, the delegates of the conference "One is the Human Spirit" propose that the time is ripe for the religions of the world to bring together in concert their several visions in aid of the United Nations in its endeavor to build a better human society. To this end, we strongly recommend that the United Nations consider the creation of an agency that will bring the much-needed resources and inspirations of the spiritual traditions to the solution of world problems.

Although the recommendation was not adopted, it remains as a guide and source of hope.

A Personal Reflection

In reflecting on that remarkable year in my life, I ask myself the question: what did I learn from this year of involvement with the UN? To paraphrase the seventeenth century English poet John Dunne, no person and no religion is an island. We are part of the whole. Increasingly so in the lens of the UN, no one and no event is isolated. From a scientific viewpoint, over half a century ago Einstein said that "a human being is part of the whole, called by us 'universe.'" In his book, Science and the Akashic Field: An Integral Theory of Everything, *the philosopher-scientist Ervin Laszlo*[146] makes the claim that the experience of our thoughts and feelings "as separate from the rest" is an "optical delusion of . . . consciousness" which creates a prison for us. The vision of the Temple of Understanding sought to break through this isolated vision, which especially marginalizes the entire spiritual realm. The problem is complicated on one hand by secularization and on the other by isolation. More than ever we are aware that we, individually and collectively, in Dunne's words, are "a piece of the continent," thus a part of a cosmos. What happens to one happens to all. However we separate church and state, our task is to build an organic spiritual community.

For those who work in interreligious dialogue, this is the compelling task of our time and of the future of the human race. Remembering again the words of Thomas Merton, "we are already one, but we imagine we are not. What we have to recover is our original unity," we must continue to bring forth the spiritual realization and the full consciousness of our already existing oneness.

UNESCO Conference on Teilhard de Chardin, Paris
September 16–18, 1981

After the United Nations Conference of world religious leaders in 1975,136 I continued to reflect on the issues that had emerged there. In 1981 I had the opportunity to explore these issues further in a talk I gave at a conference at UNESCO in Paris which celebrated the hundredth anniversary of the birth of Pierre Teilhard de Chardin. What follows here are some excerpts from that talk which are at the very root of my understanding of interreligious dialogue.

According to Pierre Teilhard de Chardin, the human community is undergoing a radical transformation of consciousness. We are evolving from a state of tribal-national awareness to global consciousness. Through a process which he calls "planetization," the forces of evolution have shifted from divergence to convergence.[147] When humankind first appeared on the earth, groups diverged into separate tribal units. However, the spherical shape of the earth, the increase in population and the rapid development of communication in recent times have caused consciousness to converge and intensify. Out of this process, global consciousness is emerging. What effect will this have on religion? What role will religion play in the process of planetization?

Teilhard sees consciousness emerging out of a process that has its roots in the geosphere and the biosphere. Throughout the process a single dynamic is at work, which he articulates as the law of "complexity-consciousness" and "union differentiates."[148] "In any domain," he says, "whether it be the cells of a body, the members of a society, or the elements of a spiritual synthesis—union differentiates." From subatomic particles to global consciousness, individual elements unite in a center-to-center union which releases creative energy leading to more complex units. The greater complexity leads to increased interiority, which makes possible more intimate creative unions. In this process the elements do not lose their identity but rather have it intensified by the union. The more "other" they become in conjunction, the more they find themselves as "self."[149] As these differentiated unions become more complex, interiority is increased and energy is released towards the formation of a more complex and interiorized consciousness. "Regarded along its axis of complexity," Teilhard states, "the universe is, both on the whole and at each of its points, in a continual tension of organic doubling-back upon itself, and thus of interiorization."[150] At this point in history, the forces of planetization are bringing about an unprecedented complexification of what Teilhard terms the noosphere, or sphere of consciousness, through the convergence of cultures and religions.

In order to see these issues in perspective, I will sketch my own understanding of the evolution of religious consciousness, drawing from Teilhard's theory of the noosphere and Karl Jaspers' theory of the Axial Period.[151]

I believe that Teilhard's general theory of evolution of consciousness can be nuanced by Karl Jaspers' description of the transformation of consciousness that occurred in the first millennium BC. Jaspers discovers an axis at this "point in history which gave birth to everything which, since then, man has been able to be." Jaspers goes on to claim that "this axis of history is to be found in the period around 500 BC, in the spiritual process that occurred between 800 and 200 BC. It is there that we meet with the most deep-cut dividing line in history. Man, as we know him today, came into being. For short we may style this the 'Axial Period'."[152]

In Greece, Israel, India and China, consciousness was transformed without discernible influence of one area on another. In China, Confucius and Lao-tze taught, and the schools of Chinese philosophy came into being; India produced the Upanishads and the wisdom of Buddhism commenced; in Israel the prophets Elijah, Isaiah and Jeremiah spurred their people to moral awakening; and in Greece, Socrates, Plato and Aristotle ushered in critical reflective thought. The great religions of the world, as we know them today, are a product of this transformation of consciousness; for Hinduism, Buddhism, Taoism, Confucianism and Judaism were shaped in this period, and the transformation of Jewish consciousness became the base for the later emergence of Christianity and Islam.

I believe that we are presently going through a Second Axial Period, which Teilhard discerned although he did not use the term. Like the First, this period has been developing for several centuries, and has reached a critical point in the twentieth. And like the First, it is effecting a radical transformation of consciousness. While the First produced individual, self-reflective consciousness, the Second period is producing global consciousness. The consciousness of the Second Axial Period is global in two senses: (1) in encompassing the entire human community on the planet in all of its historical experience; (2) in recovering its rootedness in the earth.

According to Teilhard, religion should activate and energize human creative potential in building the earth and developing the human community. In our converging context, the different religions will face the issues from their own perspectives and with their own resources. They will not speak of Christ the way Teilhard did; yet they may discern in their own tradition what Teilhard meant by the Cosmic Christ.

In the context of the Second Axial Period, then, Teilhard's thought has a special meaning for the religious phenomenon of our time. He is a prophet calling us to a moral awakening—unprecedented in human history—to take collective responsibility for the future, for the survival of life on our planet, for the evolutionary process itself. But more than this, he is a spiritual guide, for he shows us the way by pointing out the stages of the spiritual journey. From Teilhard's perspective, the spiritual journey is no longer embedded in the cosmic processes as it was in the Pre-Axial Period, nor is it a mere journey away from the cosmos and into mind as in the First Axial Period; rather the cosmos itself is on a spiritual journey as an integral process of geogenesis, biogenesis and noogenesis as stages of a single cosmic-spiritual journey. The religious phenomenon of our time represents a stage of enlightenment along this spiritual journey, when in the Second Axial Period consciousness becomes truly global by encompassing the planet and assimilating its roots in the earth.
Religious Publishing and Interreligious Dialogue

At the same period in which I gave the talk in Paris on Teilhard de Chardin, I was getting increasingly involved in religious publishing. I remember very vividly how, in the mid-seventies, I received a phone call from Richard Payne, who was then an editor at Paulist Press. "What do you think," he asked, "about developing at Paulist a series of books entitled "The Classics of Western Mysticism"? I responded very positively since over the two previous years I had begun teaching courses on Christian mysticism in the Theology Department at Fordham University and received a positive response from the students. So we began, but before we advanced very far, we changed the title of the series to The Classics of Western Spirituality, since this term could include both the highest realm of consciousness and the earlier stages leading to that goal. We started identifying texts and prospective editors of volumes who would also serve as translators.

Richard told me how he came upon the idea for the series. Each day as he took the Long Island commuter train at Amityville to his office at Paulist Press in Manhattan, he watched the trains going from east to west and others from west to east. One day the idea struck him that this movement of the trains was like the coming of spiritual teachers from the East to the West and the movement of Western spiritual seekers going from the West to the East.

As an editor he felt drawn to meet this awakening of the spirit by the series The Classics of Western Spirituality in 60 volumes.[153] By he included Judaism, Christianity, Islam, and Native American spi

At the same time, Richard conceived of two more series. Th entitled World Spirituality: An Encyclopedic History of the Relig in 25 volumes, 500 pages each, with about 20 articles along v describing the spiritual wisdom and practice of the tradition. dimension of the project has been that the editors and contributors from the specific tradition, with very few exceptions. In the e Richard asked me to be the General Editor of this series. It was that Richard moved to Crossroad Press and took the World Spiritu with him.

For about a year Richard and I spent one day a week developing structure of the volumes: identifying an editor or a team of editors f volumes, and seeking advice from specialists from around the w the team of editors was in place, we solicited for each volume a list of and contributors.

As this structure began taking shape, I realized that we had in the twenty or so editors a unique community that could meet from time to time to share their vision. The editors met on two occasions for a public conference at Fordham University on "World Spirituality: The Meeting of Spiritual Paths," in 1983 and 1990. They also met for two conferences at the United Nations on "Interreligious Dialogue and World Peace," in 1984 and 1986. Later they met six times at the East–West Center in Honolulu, on the relation of the indigenous people of the Pacific Rim and the editors represented in the World Spirituality series. Several editors represented the series at a special session at the Parliament of the World's Religions in Barcelona, July 7–13, 2004, on "World Spirituality: Into the Future." Of the volumes in the series, eighteen have been published. Plans are being made for a meeting of the editors along with others on the climactic volume of the series: World Spirituality: Into the Future.

When Richard Payne had his "epiphany" at the Long Island Railroad station, he conceived a plan to publish three series, a third being The Classics of Eastern Spirituality. One hundred years ago such a series was published by Oxford University Press under the title The Sacred Books of the East. There is agreement that after one hundred years there should be a new version of The Sacred Books of the East. Richard has prepared a revised list and hopes to find a publisher in the near future.

The two existing series along with the proposed revision of The Sacred Books of the East would represent the most powerful resource for mutual understanding and dialogue among the world religions that we have at the present and into the future.

Passage to India

After my talk at UNESCO and my increasing involvement in religious publishing, in the fall of 1981 I began what has been my richest experience of interreligious dialogue. Over an eight year period, I traveled to India more than ten times and plunged ever more deeply into the vast world of Hinduism. Each trip lasted about three weeks, involving travel to the major cities of India: Bombay (Mumbai), Delhi, Calcutta, and Madras. This travel also included two trips to Cochin on the southwest coast and three to Varansi (Banaras) in the north as well as three to Nepal.

My passage to India involved the same approach of "passing over and coming back" that I described in my previous installment on my contact with the Sioux Indians in South Dakota and Muslims in the Middle East: (1) to immerse myself in the total concrete life world of some followers of a religion; (2) with the plan to participate empathetically in that consciousness; (3) to return enriched to my own.

This stage of my journey into interreligious dialogue began with an invitation to participate in a conference in Cochin on "The Religions of India." The participants included 300 from India and 50 from other countries. The conference was very strategic for me since without it I would have taken years on my own to meet so many participants who reflected the richness and diversity of India.

One of the first things I observed was that Christianity was an ancient religion in India, with roots that go back continuously to the third century if not earlier. Another fact was graphically illustrated at the conference: that Buddhism was originally an ancient religion in India but eventually moved to far East Asia. There were only five Buddhists present: two from Tibet, two from Sri Lanka, and one from Bombay, who was a convert from Hinduism. About eighty percent of the population of India is Hindu, and nearly twelve percent Muslim. Throughout the seven days of the conference, I was able to experience the rich dynamic of the different groups: Hindus, Muslims, Jains, Sikks, Zoroastrians, and Christians, which made me feel at home among the religions of India. Not far from our conference was a small colony of Jews who trace their origin in India back more than two thousand years. Through the papers and discussions, prayers, and rituals, the conference provided concrete experiences of the rich religious diversity of India, and at the same time revealed the pervasive presence of Hinduism.

Throughout I was much involved in the many facets of the conference as a participant in the discussion, presenter of a paper, and as a member of the committee which formulated the joint statement read at the final session. All of this was richly surrounded by a lush tropical setting of palm trees, inhabited by friendly monkeys. Each evening there were cultural events of classical Indian music, and scenes depicted from the great Hindu epics. All in all, the conference provided an ideal introduction to my passage to India. With this introduction I was well equipped to explore the ever unfolding cultural and spiritual richness of India. Before leaving Cochin, I was able to visit the birthplace and shrine of Sánkara, considered by many to be the greatest theologian-philosopher of Hinduism.

The Burning Ghats

The most moving of all cities for me was Varanasi (or Banaras) named after two rivers flowing into the Ganges—the Varuna and the Asi. It is to the plain between these rivers that millions of Hindus come to die and have their bodies cremated and their ashes cast into the Ganges. Across the river lies the emptiness and silence of "the other shore." To be present at the cremation ceremony is an overwhelming experience that defies articulation. Among the countless religious ceremonies in the world, the cremation of the bodies of devout Hindus on the banks of the Ganges touches the essence of the human situation at a depth beyond all words. It is abrupt, stark, yet surrounded by chanting—it is inevitable and at the same time profoundly transcending.

In Varanasi I usually stayed with a friend at Asi Ghat. The term "ghat" refers to the ceremonial stairs which pilgrims descend for ritual bathing in the Ganges. My room was at the side of the Ganges, and every morning beginning about 3:30 A.M. I could hear the pilgrims chanting as they progressed along the narrow path below. In this setting the sun rises dramatically over the Ganges. The power of the sunrise over the Ganges echoes in the West. Dante describes the birth of St. Francis as reflecting the sun rising over the Ganges.

A short distance north of Varanasi is Sarnath, one of the holiest sites of Buddhism, for it is here that the Buddha preached his first sermon and gathered his disciples. It was here that Buddhist monasticism was born. Numerous groups of Buddhists have established centers here. The serene atmosphere of the setting is in sharp contrast to the turmoil of Varanasi and the burning ghats of the Ganges.

On one occasion, Krishna Sivarama, the editor of the Hindu volumes in the World Spirituality series, suggested that I visit the Maharaja of Varanasi and request that he join the editorial board of the World Spirituality series. I met him in one of his palaces across the Ganges and was most cordially received. He very graciously accepted. I also took the occasion to describe the initiative that had emerged out of the Temple of Understanding conference at the United Nations in 1975 concerning establishing a center for the meeting of world religious leaders on world peace. The idea had surfaced again at the UNESCO conference in 1981 but lacked funding. The Maharaja expressed enthusiastic support. "In fact," he said, "you can have one of my palaces for that purpose." I had never dreamed that one day a maharaja would offer me one of his palaces. However, unfortunately, this dream did not come to pass.

While in Varanasi, I had the opportunity of meeting with Bithika Murkerji, one of the editors of the Hindu volumes of World Spirituality, of which I am the General Editor. We met with a group of contributors on the campus of Banaras Hindu University where she was a professor of philosophy. She had gathered about fifteen contributors who were writing articles for the two Hindu volumes. For some time we discussed editorial matters of style. After a while I raised a question to Bithika and the group. When they turned in the outline of their volumes, they presented the topics in chronological order beginning with the Vedic period, then the Upanishads. This, I said, somewhat surprised me since we in the West tend to think of the Hindus as not experiencing unilinear time as flow as the West does.

This opened a deep discussion on the meaning of time. It brought back my days on the Sioux reservation in South Dakota when the issue of time was central. Clearly, the Hindus are not indigenous people, although there are more than a million indigenous people living in India, many in the mountains where I have had the occasion to meet some of them. However, the Hindus belong to the Axial Period with its distinctive form of consciousness, especially in the realm of time. Bithika went on to explain that the Hindus have divided time in a way that on the surface corresponds with the West. But on a deeper experienced level she, for example, perceived time as organic—"all at once," she said. As she put it, "I study the Vedas and the Upanishads and the Bhagavad Gita, but I experience them as all one."

This issue has great significance for the human community. Time is not visible, but our cultural understanding of time controls our lives. Issues such as these emerge when we enter into contact with other cultures, spiritually or pragmatically. In this era, as global encounters are becoming more pervasive, our awareness of the different experiences of time on our planet can lead more creatively into the emerging global community.

Journey South: University of Madras

Krishna Sivaraman, the editor of the Hindu volumes of the *World Spirituality* series, strongly suggested that I visit R. Balasubramanian, the assistant editor, who was in charge of articles originating from the Tamil country of South India, chiefly Madras.

After traveling to the south, I met him in his office at the university that overlooked the sea and one of the largest and most scenic beaches in the world. As we looked out at the sea, we chatted for sometime about his role as editor. At one point he handed me an offprint of an article he had written on one of the Tamil mystics of southern India. I read the article hurriedly and was gripped by the fact that Balo, as he asked me to call him, was using the same method of phenomenology that I used in my study of mysticism. I turned to him and suggested that he and I jointly write a book entitled Mysticism: Hindu and Christian. He would write chapters on Shankhara and Ramanuja and I would write chapters on Eckhart and Bonaventure. We agreed, and he invited me to return to India the next year to give a series of lectures at the Radhakrishnan Institute for the Advanced Study of Philosophy, of which Balo was the director. This began a collaboration that has lasted for many years.

I returned the next year to Madras and gave the lectures to a group of some 60 graduate students, most of them from India. These talks were subsequently published under the title Global Spirituality: Toward the Meeting of Spiritual Paths.[155] We agreed on a common methodology and continued our discussions when I returned to the University of Madras to give another series of lectures the following year. We have also met in Europe and the United States, where I invited him to lecture in my class at Columbia University. We would have completed the project, but he was given a new post at Pondicherry. However, we continue to be in touch and hope to complete this project in the near future. This is an example of the kind of in-depth mutual explorations that can emerge in this age of interreligious dialogue.

In my several trips to Madras, I was not only the guest of Balo at the University but of the family of one of my close friends and collaborators who teaches in the U.S. and is from Madras, K.R. Sundararajan. I was also the guest of his sister and her husband, who took me to explore not only the magnificent art museum in Madras, but also the Christian sites such as the Church of the Apostle Thomas, who brought Christianity to India in the first century.

Calcutta: G.D. Birla and Mother Teresa

During my years of travel in India, I visited Calcutta five times. Overflowing with more than thirteen million people, Calcutta is a city of opposites. Once the shining gem in the British crown, Calcutta was the capital of India during the British Empire until 1910. It is now notorious for its poverty and for its teeming millions who sleep on its sidewalks or in its huge train station. On my visits to Calcutta, I was exposed to its poverty and to its wealth.

Through my connection with Juliet Hollister and the Temple of Understanding, I was often a guest at the home of the Birla family, who alternately vied with the Tatas to be the wealthiest family in India. The head of the Birla family, G. D. Birla, was Mahatma Gandhi's chief benefactor. It was at the Birla home in Delhi that Gandhi was assassinated. The Birla estate is now a national monument.

On several occasions I was a guest of the Birla family in Calcutta. They provided me with a car and a driver who took me on a very extensive tour of Calcutta, which included going to the shrine of Ramakrishna on the bank of a tributary of the Ganges. Once I was a dinner guest when the family hosted a major spiritual teacher who resided in the Himalayas. From him I learned firsthand of his life of meditation in that remarkable setting.

The year before G.D. Birla's death, his family went with him on a pilgrimage to Gangotri, the ritual source of the Ganges River, in the foothills of the Himalayas. It was a difficult journey for him, but he walked the narrow path with the religious fervor that permeated his life.

His family made a video of his pilgrimage and they asked me if I would also interview him for a family video on his life. What an honor! It was a privilege to interview this great leader whose life played such a central role in the history of India. He was Gandhi's major disciple and benefactor and a leading figure in the development of the independence of India. In our interview I asked him about his role in the international scene, particularly his contact with Winston Churchill and Franklin Roosevelt, and his own view of the future of India. It was a privilege to meet this great man, who was looked upon by many as a saint. Each morning when he took walks near his home, crowds would gather round him to seek his spiritual advice. He had a great reputation, not only in political and financial affairs, but also in spiritual wisdom.

Over several generations the Birla family has built major temples, notably the great Birla Temple in Delhi, opened by Gandhi in 1938 to people of all castes and religions. The family has sponsored interreligious events such as the well-known Calcutta conference where Thomas Merton made his now-famous statement: "My dear Brothers and Sisters, we are already one, but we imagine we are not. What we have to recover is our original unity: what we have to be is what we already are."

The Birlas have also been close friends and benefactors of Mother Teresa. In fact, when our planning committee for the UN conference wanted to invite Mother to speak at the UN, Juliet Hollister asked Sarala Birla, G.D. Birla's daughter-in-law, to go personally to Mother Teresa's center and to invite her to come to the UN.

I would like to turn now to Mother Teresa. She devoted her life to work for "the poorest of the poor" in Calcutta. This work brought her recognition not only in Calcutta, but around the world for her dedication to bringing dignity to those suffering the most abject poverty. Her compassion and love have inspired the world. For this she was awarded the Nobel Peace Prize. It has been my privilege to meet her on a number of occasions in India, but the highpoint for me was at the United Nations headquarters in New York. At the closing session of the Temple of Understanding Conference, October 24, 1975, I had the honor of formally introducing her to an audience of delegates from around the world. I can say without exaggeration that her presentation was the most profound and moving talk that I have ever heard.

On my trips to Calcutta, I had the privilege to visit with Mother Teresa, attend Mass at her convent, and speak with her personally about her work with the poor. I also visited her home for the dying on the edge of the temple of Kali, the fearsome goddess so revered by devotees in Calcutta. Mother Teresa described her work very movingly when she spoke at the United Nations. She told of a man who lay in the gutter and had been brought to the home for the dying. "He said he'd lived like an animal, but would die like an angel with love and care." It is this profound compassion that can change the world.

In thinking over my contact with G.D. Birla and Mother Teresa, I reflected on the different focus of their life's work: G.D. Birla in building the economic and political structure of modern India, out of the deepest spiritual commitment—and Mother Teresa, bringing compassion and love to the dying on the streets of Calcutta. In the larger scheme of things, their monumental contributions—in Calcutta, India, and the world—touch and ignite each other. India can embrace them both!

The Mystical Himalayas

On my first trip to India, I flew from Calcutta to Delhi. Off to my right, I could see at a great distance the wall of the snow-capped Himalayas shining in the sunlight. This moved me very deeply. Since I was a young boy, I was gripped by the majesty of mountains, but at the same time I had never seen one, for I grew up in New Orleans, which is as much as fifteen feet below sea level, with no hills, much less mountains. One night when I was eight years old, I dreamt of Mount Everest, only to wake up in the morning to realize my plight. I was "mountain deprived!" Since then I have been drawn to hills and mountains, and in a special way to the Himalayas. So when I had glimpsed the Himalayas between Calcutta and Delhi, I made plans in my mind to fly the next year to Kathmandu in Nepal where I would be encompassed by the Himalayas.

So the next year, when I returned to India, I flew from Delhi to Varanasi and from there went on to Kathmandu, the capital of Nepal. I was so drawn by the majesty of the Himalayas and the exotic quality of Kathmandu that eventually I returned to Kathmandu three times in one calendar year.

As I traveled in India, I was struck by the way my Hindu friends spoke of the Himalayas as a symbol of the heights of the spiritual journey. It is true that the Himalayas are vast and to a large measure inaccessible. But there is more— for they have a silent grandeur that hovers between earth and heaven and beckons the spiritual seeker to rise to realms of overwhelming majesty. I had found glimpses of this in the Alps at Mount Blanc where I camped with my family and also in the Rocky Mountains in the Western United States. But the Himalayas have a unique attraction that symbolizes to spiritual seekers East and West the heights, the depth, and the grandeur of the spiritual journey.

When I landed in Kathmandu and checked in at passport control, I signed my name as Hilary Cousins, using my middle name, after Sir Edmund Hillary, who with Tenzing Norgay was the first to climb Mount Everest in 1947. Once through passport control, I took a cab through the crowded streets to a hotel named Tibet Guest House. When we turned the corners, I got glimpses of the massive snow white peaks of the Himalayas. On the congested streets I saw the mountain people of Nepal and Tibet, who conveyed a silent majesty like the mountains overhead. I said to myself spontaneously, "This is the most exotic place I have ever been." Finally, we stopped at the hotel and I settled in for the night—under heavy blankets.

Leaving Kathmandu the next morning, we flew along the Himalayas until we came to what appeared to be an opening in the wall of the mountains. It revealed, as it were, a royal court comprised of two mountain—Nuptse and Lhotse—as if they were mighty courtiers in the service of their king. In the center of this court, Mount Everest appeared in solemn grandeur—with a wisp of clouds streaming from its peak—standing in awesome majesty as the mighty Monarch of the World.

When I traveled on a later occasion, the sky was so clear that in the distance I could see Kangchenjunga, the third highest mountain in the world, shining in the sun. The second highest mountain, K2, known locally as "Chogu Ri" or "The Great Mountain," is far to the west and out of sight.

The flight back to Kathmandu was riveting as we flew so close to the Himalayas that it seemed we could almost touch the mountains. Then the pilots invited the passengers to come to the cockpit, where it seemed that we could actually step onto the mountains and touch with our hands the massive wall of gray granite with white snow streaming down its slopes. As we neared Kathmandu, we could see farther to the West the mountain named Anapurna, over 26 thousand feet high. The power of these mountains is overwhelming. In their silence they thunder the grandeur of God.

In Tibet and in Nepal the Buddhists revere Mount Everest as sacred. Two monasteries were built nearby just to contemplate the mountain. Rongphu Monastery in Tibet, below the Rongphu glacier, was built by the Nyingma Lama, and is the highest monastery in the world. It is considered by experts to be the best place to view Mount Everest. Thyangboche monastery in the Khumbu Valley, with its high lama, is a place of worship with mystical chanting, music, and contemplation of the mountain.

The Tibetan name for Mount Everest is "Mount Qomolangma" or "Chomolungma," Mother Goddess of the Earth" or "Mother Goddess of the Snows." In Nepal the name is "Sagarmatha," "Mother Goddess of the Sky" or "Forehead of the Sky." The Tibetan and Nepali names have both been translated as "Mother Goddess of the Universe." As these names would tell us, the highest mountain in the world is a place where earth and heaven meet, a mingling of the created universe and of the divine.

Here in the high Himalayas my journey reached a certain completion— the conclusion of a major stage of the spiritual journey that I had begun on the Sioux Reservation in South Dakota some thirty years before. But my larger journey did not come to a final end in the heights of the Himalayas. It continued down the mountainside and into the future.

Kaleidoscope: To the Far East

My travel eventually encircled the earth three times. In the late eighties and early nineties, I began focusing on Far East Asia and Buddhism. I visited Korea twice—to attend conferences that dealt with Taoism and Buddhism. I also met in Japan with Takeuchi Yoshinori, the editor of the two Buddhist volumes of World Spirituality and with the editorial committee that had been formed at the Nanzan Institute for Religion and Culture in Nagoya. I traveled to South East Asia, chiefly to Thailand, to connect with Buddhism there. With our Confucian editor, Tu Wei-ming, I helped organize six conferences on the indigenous people of the Pacific Rim in dialogue with the editors of the *World Spirituality* volumes. For me personally, this was a return to roots, since it was my contacts with the Sioux Indians in South Dakota, more than forty years ago, that drew me into interreligious dialogue.

In the mid-nineties, I had the extraordinary opportunity of taking part in the Gethsemani Encounter between Buddhist and Christian monks and nuns. This was the high point of my journey into interreligious dialogue. I am still in the glow of that extraordinary event.

I would like to close with a quotation from my long-time friend Fr. Robley Whitson. We taught together for a number of years at Fordham University and are presently colleagues at the Graduate Theological Foundation, of which he is the founder. I believe his statement touches the very heart of interreligious dialogue.

The Coming Convergence of World Religions:
Robley Whitson

The question before us, then, is not whether the world's religious traditions have a positive significance for one another, but rather, how we can formulate an understanding of that significance. The formulation we seek must arise from within actual religious experience and be capable of speaking to one who listens from within a tradition of sharing specific historic forms of experience. It must not presume that the process towards unity will destroy the various traditions, reducing them to some common, indeterminate kind of religious experience. On the contrary, to be authentic it must recognize and prize the very different heritages, for we can now see that each at its core is unique. Somehow the differing traditions, originating in isolation from each other and so coming to their present maturity separately, are to become dimensions of one another, complementing each other by their varied uniqueness, and making possible an undreamed of breadth and depth of vision for the human race in an infinite universe.[156]

Chapter 11
Global Spirituality

The term "global spirituality" reflects one of the major religious phenomena of our time. Over the last hundred years there has emerged an increasing interest in world religions, not primarily in terms of their history and doctrines, but in terms of their spiritual wisdom that can enrich and guide seekers on their individual spiritual journey and at the same time lead to the emergence of a global spiritual community. This is a matter of great challenge and opportunity, for as Philip Sheldrake observes, "The self-identity of Christian spirituality is in the process of a massive transition as it comes to terms with existence in a global, multi-cultural, multi-faith world."

In his book, *The Way of All the Earth*, John Dunne writes: "Is a religion coming to birth in our time? It could be. What seems to be occurring is a phenomenon we might call 'passing over,' passing over from one culture to another, from one way of life to another, from one religion to another. According to Dunne, passing over leads to a return: "It is followed by an equal and opposite process we might call 'coming back,' coming back with a new insight to one's own culture, one's own way of life, one's own religion." Dunne sees this process as characteristic: "Passing over and coming back, it seems, is the spiritual adventure of our time."

The meaning of the two terms in our topic "global" and "spirituality" can be seen through the perspective of a 25-volume publishing project entitled *World Spirituality: An Encyclopedic History of the Religious Quest*. In terms of scope this project covers the vast history of spirituality from prehistoric times into the traditions of Asia, Europe, Africa, Australia, and North and South America. Although it focuses also on the present and the future, it encompasses the whole of human history. In describing the nature of spirituality, it proposes the following definition:

The series focuses on that inner dimension of the person called by certain traditions "the spirit." This spiritual core is the deepest center of the person. It is here that the person is open to the transcendent dimension; it is here that the person experiences ultimate reality. The series explores the discovery of this core, the dynamics of its development, and its journey to the ultimate goal. It deals with prayer, spiritual direction, the various maps of the spiritual journey, and the methods of advancement in the spiritual ascent.

The meaning of global spirituality can also be seen through the lens of the Parliament of the World's Religions, which held its first meeting in Chicago in 1893. It was at this gathering that Swami Vivekananda electrified a large audience and effectively launched the interreligious movement. Throughout the next century the movement increased around the world and eventually gained such momentum that many thought the interreligious movement had become global and there was no need for a Parliament in Chicago. However, it was decided to hold a hundredth anniversary meeting of the Parliament, which took place in Chicago in 1993, with some eight thousand attending. It was at this event that a suggestion was made to hold meetings about every five years. As a result, the next meeting was in Capetown in 1999 with almost eight thousand attending and most recently in Barcelona with almost nine thousand. The interreligious movement has now become global, with meetings held increasingly throughout the world, supported by numerous publications.

By looking at the plan of the most recent Parliament in Barcelona, we can get a picture of its scope and content. The Barcelona Parliament took place over one week and consisted of a plenary session each evening along with a total of more than 700 sessions throughout the week, covering the wide range of global spirituality. For example, one session involved a Hindu, Sundarararjan, a Confucian, Tu Weiming, and a Christian, Ramon Panikkar on the topic: "World Spirituality: Into the Future." Another session was on "Praying Together" with Marcus Braybrook, President of the World Congress of Faiths, Iman Dr. Abdul Jalil, and Fr. Albert Nambiaparambil.

In order to understand the present and future unfolding of spirituality, it is valuable to situate it in its historical context. The history of spirituality can be expressed in three periods:

1. **Pre-Axial Period.** The first stage of human consciousness is what existed among indigenous people before the emergence of Axial consciousness.

2. **The Axial Period.** (So named because it was the axis around which history turned.) After along development of agriculture, river trade, and communication through the use of the alphabet and written texts, a new kind of consciousness emerged: Axial consciousness, which appeared in Asia and Europe between 800 and 200 BC. Axial consciousness itself, as well as those other developments, provided the basis for the civilizations of the world, along with the emergence of the great world religions: Hinduism, Buddhism, Taoism, Confucianism, Judaism, and later Christianity and Islam.

3. The Second Axial Period began its emergence about 1900. It is the
period in which we now find ourselves, and it continues into the future.

My understanding of these periods is derived from Teilhard de Chardin's
general theory of the evolution of consciousness, with the shift from divergence
to convergence taking place in our era.

This global consciousness, complexified through the meeting of cultures
and religions, is only one characteristic of the Second Axial Period. The
consciousness of this period is global in another sense, namely, in rediscovering
its roots in the earth. At the very moment when the various cultures and
religions are meeting each other and creating a new global community, our
life on the planet is being threatened. The very tools that we have used to
bring about this convergence, industrialization and technology, are undercutting
the biological support system that sustains life on our planet. The future of
consciousness, even life on Earth, is shrouded in a cloud of uncertainty by the
pollution of our environment, the depletion of natural resources, the unjust
distribution of wealth, and the stockpiling of nuclear weapons. Unless the
human community reverses these destructive forces, we may not survive far
into the future. The human race as a whole—all the diverse cultures and
religions—must face these problems squarely.

In the Second Axial Period we must rediscover the dimensions of
consciousness of the spirituality of the primal peoples of the Pre-Axial Period.
As we saw, this consciousness was collective and cosmic, rooted in the earth
and the life cycles. We must rapidly appropriate that form of consciousness or
perish. I am not suggesting, however, a romantic attempt to live in the past,
but that the evolution of consciousness proceeds by way of recapitulation.
Having developed self-reflective, analytic, critical consciousness in the First
Axial Period, we must now, while retaining these values, reappropriate and
integrate into that consciousness the collective and cosmic dimensions of the
pre-Axial consciousness. We must recapture the unity of tribal consciousness
by seeing humanity as a single tribe, and we must see this single tribe related
organically to the total cosmos. This means that the consciousness of the
twenty-first century will be global from two perspectives: from a horizontal
perspective, cultures and religions must meet each other on the surface of the
globe, entering into creative encounters that will produce a complexified
collective consciousness; and from a vertical perspective, they must plunge
their roots deep into the earth in order to provide a stable and secure base for
future development.

This new global consciousness must be organically ecological, supported by structures that will ensure justice and peace. The voices of the oppressed—the poor, women, and racial and ethnic minorities—must be heard and heeded. These groups, along with the earth itself, can be looked upon as the prophets and teachers of the Second Axial Period. This emerging twofold global consciousness is not just a creative possibility to enhance the twenty-first century; it is an absolute necessity if we are to survive.

What does this mean for religions in the twenty-first century? It means that they have a double task: to enter creatively into the dialogue of religions and to channel their energies into solving the common human problems that threaten our future on the earth. It means that they must strip away negative and limiting attitudes toward other religions. They must avoid both a narrow fundamentalism and a bland universalism. They must be true to their spiritual heritage, for this is the source of their power and their gift to the world. They must make every effort to ground themselves in their own traditions and at the same time to open themselves to other traditions. In concert with the other religions they should commit themselves to creating the new complexified global consciousness we have been exploring.

But to meet, even creatively, on the spiritual level is not enough. They must channel their spiritual resources toward the solution of global problems. For the most part, this calls for a transformation of the religions. Having been formed in the First Axial Period, the religions bear the mark of Axial consciousness in turning toward the spiritual ascent and away from the material. The religions must rediscover the material dimension of existence and its spiritual significance. In this they can learn from the secular that justice and peace are human values that must be cherished and pragmatically cultivated. But they must not adopt an exclusively secular attitude, for their unique contribution is to tap their reservoirs of spiritual energy and channel this into developing secular enterprises that are genuinely human. I believe that it is in this larger context that the emerging spiritual communities of the world must face together the challenges of the Second Axial Period.

In conclusion, the roots of global spirituality go back to the dawn of human history. From the very beginning, in spite of differences, it has had a common core which emerged in diverse ways throughout the unfolding of history. In our era, with increasing communication and with the convergence of cultures, we are beginning to awaken to the fact that we have been on a single spiritual journey from the very outset.

REFERENCES

Series: *Classics of Western Spirituality*, 106 vols (Christian, Jewish, Muslim) (Mahwah, NJ: Paulist Press, 1978—; *World Spirituality: An Encyclopedic History of the Religious Quest*, ed. Ewert Cousins, 25 vols. (New York: Crossroad, 1985—.

John Dunne, *The Way of All the Earth: Experiments in Truth and Religion* (Notre Dame: University of Notre Dame Press, 1978); Raimundo Panikkar, *The Trinity and the Religious Experience of Man* (New York: Orbis Books, 1973).
Religions of the World
Facing the Future Together

Chapter 12
Religions of the World Facing the Furture Together

At the outset, I would like to clarify my understanding of the situation in which the religions of the world find themselves. Are they facing modernity? Or postmodernity? Or even a greater challenge? I believe they are facing a greater challenge than modernity or postmodernity. In fact, as I will develop below, I believe that this is the greatest challenge that has confronted the human race in its entire history.

All the religions—and all the peoples of the world—are undergoing the most radical, far-reaching, and challenging transformation in history. The stakes are high: the very survival of life on our planet; either chaos and destruction, or creative transformation and the birth of a new consciousness. Forces, which have been at work for centuries, have in our day reached a crescendo that has the power to draw the human race into a global network and the religions of the world into a global spiritual community.

Modernity and Postmodernity

Can this transformation be called modernity? Yes, if modernity is taken in the most general sense to mean our present situation. However, the term "modernity," as it has been used, carries other meanings and connotations. It has come to mean the intellectual and cultural heritage of Western science and the Age of Enlightenment. As such, it includes the empirical-rational mindset derived from scientific research, our industrial-technological lifestyle, the free-market economy, and the political ideals of individual human rights and democracy. Over the last 400 years, Judaism and Christianity—and, more recently, Islam—have had to grapple with the forces of modernity, critically assimilating some of its values and at the same time striving to maintain their religious heritage against modernity's thrust toward secularization.

Over the last decade the mindset of modernity, especially in its scientific enterprise, has been radically challenged in intellectual circles. In its place there has arisen "postmodernity," a cluster of attitudes and positions that have turned away from science's passionate search for a unified truth about the material world and have concerned themselves with an endless examination of human expressions in texts and cultural forms. Closely connected with this is an affirmation of pluralism in the form of multiculturalism and the emerging voices of the oppressed.

In this essay I am making the claim that both modernity's search for unity and postmodernity's affirmation of pluralism reflect aspects of our present cultural and religious situation. However, neither provides the whole picture. At least in their origins, modernity and postmodernity are Western phenomena, and our present and immediate future is a global phenomenon. I believe, therefore, that Judaism, Christianity, and Islam must face this phenomenon together; however, in so doing, they must also face it together with Hinduism, Buddhism, and the other religions of the world. Further, the West must cease reading history from within its own cultural horizons, as it usually does in tracing the origin and development of modernity and postmodernity. The forces that are bringing about our present transformation have been global from the start. It is imperative, then, that we make an attempt to see our history as a global history.

In order to do this, we must disengage ourselves from any particular culture or religion, situating ourselves at a viewing point from which we can see clearly both cultures and religions in a global perspective. In doing this we will be like the astronauts who travelled into outer space and looked back on the earth. What they saw overwhelmed them! For the first time in history, humans actually saw the earth as a whole. They saw the earth's clouds, oceans, and continents, it is true, but not as discrete elements; nor did they behold merely a limited horizon as when standing on the earth's surface. Rather, they saw the earth as an interrelated, organic whole—a single globe of remarkable beauty and unity. It is striking that, at the very moment in history when culture is becoming globalized, we have obtained our first sense-impression of the earth as a single globe. This image of the beautiful blue globe, shining against the black background of the universe and moving in its orbit in space, can concretely symbolize the emergence of global consciousness on the eve of the twenty-first century.

The Axial Period

From our astronaut's position, let us look back in history to another period when the world religions were fundamentally shaped into their present form. If we look at the earth from our distant vantage point during the first millennium BC, we would observe a remarkable phenomenon. From the period between 800 and 200 BC, peaking about 500 BC, a striking transformation of consciousness occurred around the earth in three geographic regions, apparently without the influence of one on the other. If we look at China, we will see two great teachers, Lao-tze and Confucius, from whose wisdom emerged the schools of Chinese philosophy. In India the cosmic, ritualistic Hinduism of the Vedas was being transformed by the Upanishads, while the Buddha and Mahavira ushered in two new religious traditions. If we turn our gaze farther west, we observe a similar development in the Eastern Mediterranean region. In Israel the Jewish prophets—Elijah, Isaiah, and Jeremiah—called forth from their people a new moral awareness. In Greece Western philosophy was born. The pre-Socratic cosmologists sought a rational explanation for the universe; Socrates awakened the moral consciousness of the Athenians; Plato and Aristotle developed metaphysical systems.

It was Karl Jaspers, the German philosopher, who some forty-five years ago pointed out the significance of this phenomenon in his book *The Origin and Goal of History*.[157] He called the period from 800 to 200 BC the "Axial Period" because it "gave birth to everything which, since then, man has been able to be." It is here in this period "that we meet with the most deepcut dividing line in history. Man, as we know him today, came into being. For short we may style this the 'Axial Period'."[158]

Although the leaders who effected this change were philosophers and religious teachers, the change was so radical that it affected all aspects of culture, for it transformed consciousness itself. It was within the horizons of this form of consciousness that the great civilizations of Asia, the Middle East, and Europe developed. Although within these horizons many developments occurred through the subsequent centuries, the horizons themselves did not change. It was this form of consciousness that was spread to other regions through migration and explorations, thus becoming the dominant, though not exclusive, form of consciousness in the world. To this day, whether we have been born and raised in the culture of China, India, Europe, or the Americas, we bear the structure of consciousness that was shaped in this Axial Period.

What is this structure of consciousness, and how does it differ from pre-axial consciousness? Prior to the Axial Period the dominant form of consciousness was cosmic, collective, tribal, mythic, and ritualistic. This is the characteristic form of consciousness of primal peoples. Between these traditional cultures and the Axial Period there emerged great empires in Egypt, China, and Mesopotamia, but these did not yet produce the full consciousness of the Axial Period.

The consciousness of the tribal cultures was intimately related to the cosmos and to the fertility cycles of nature. Thus there was established a rich and creative harmony between primal peoples and the world of nature, a harmony that was explored, expressed, and celebrated in myth and ritual. Just as they felt themselves part of nature, so they experienced themselves as part of the tribe. It was precisely the web of interrelationships within the tribe that sustained them psychologically, energizing all aspects of their lives. To be separated from the tribe threatened them with death, not only physical but psychological as well. However, their relation to the collectivity often did not extend beyond their own tribe, for they often looked upon other tribes as hostile. Yet, within their tribe they felt organically related to their group as a whole, to the life cycles of birth and death and to nature and the cosmos.

The Axial Period ushered in a radically new form of consciousness. Whereas primal consciousness was tribal, axial consciousness was individual. "Know thyself" became the watchword of Greece; the Upanishads identified the *atman*, the transcendent center of the self. The Buddha charted the way of individual enlightenment; the Jewish prophets awakened individual moral responsibility. This sense of individual identity, as distinct from the tribe and from nature, is the most characteristic mark of axial consciousness. From this flow other characteristics: consciousness that is self-reflective, analytic, and able to be applied to nature in the form of scientific theories, to society in the form of social critique, to knowledge in the form of philosophy, to religion in the form of mapping an individual spiritual journey. This self-reflective, analytic, critical consciousness stood in sharp contrast to primal mythic and ritualistic consciousness. When self-reflective *logos* emerged in the Axial Period, it tended to oppose the traditional *mythos*. Of course, mythic and ritualistic forms of consciousness survive in the post-Axial Period even to this day, but they are often submerged, surfacing chiefly in dreams, literature, and art.

Although axial consciousness brought many benefits, it involved loss as well. It severed the harmony with nature and the tribe. Axial persons were in possession of their own identity, it is true, but they had lost their organic relation to nature and community. They now ran the risk of being alienated from the matrix of being and life. With their new powers, they could criticize the social structure and by analysis discover the abstract laws of science and metaphysics, but they might find themselves mere spectators of a drama of which in reality they were an integral part.

The emergence of axial consciousness was decisive for religions, since it marked the divide in history where the major religions emerged and separated themselves from their primal antecedents. The great religions of the world as we know them today are the product of the Axial Period. Hinduism, Buddhism, Taoism, Confucianism, and Judaism took shape in their classical form during this period; and Judaism provided the base for the later emergence of Christianity and Islam. The common structures of consciousness found in these religions are characteristic of the general transformation of consciousness effected in the Axial Period.

Axial and Primal Spirituality

The move into axial consciousness released enormous spiritual energy. It opened up the individual spiritual path, especially the inner way in which the new subjectivity became the avenue into the transcendent. It allowed the deeper self to sort out the difference between the illusion of the phenomenal world and the authentic vision of reality. On the ethical level it allowed individual moral conscience to take a critical stand against the collectivity. Also, it made possible a link between the moral and the spiritual aspects of the self, so that a path could be charted through virtues toward the ultimate goal of the spiritual quest.

One of the most distinctive forms of spirituality that became available in the Axial Period was monasticism. Although it had roots in the earlier Hindu tradition, it emerged in a clearly defined way in Buddhism and Jainism at the peak of the Axial Period and later developed in Christianity. Monasticism did not exist among primal peoples, because their consciousness was not oriented to sustain it. Axial consciousness was grounded in a distinct center of individuality necessary to produce the monk as a religious type. For, the monks and nuns themselves take a radical stand as marginal persons, separating themselves from family and community, stripping themselves of material goods by practicing poverty, and withdrawing from the fertility cycles by celibacy— as wandering beggars or as members of monastic communities who share their sense of radicalness.

Although axial consciousness opened many possibilities, it tended to close off others and to produce some negative results. The release of spiritual energy thrust the axial person in the direction of the spirit and away from the earth, away from the life cycles and the harmony with nature, which the primal peoples experienced and which they made the basis of their spirituality. In some traditions this emergence of spiritual energy caused a radical split between the phenomenal world and true reality, between matter and spirit, between earth and heaven. Although in a number of traditions this separation was not central, nevertheless, the emergence of axial consciousness, with its strong sense of subjectivity, made that separation not only possible but also a risk and a threat. From the time of the Axial Period, the spiritual path tended to lead away from the earth and toward the heavenly realms above.

Note that I am placing the radical transformation of consciousness in the first millennium BC and not at the rise of Western science in the Renaissance and the Age of Enlightenment. It is, of course, true that Western science was innovative, even radical. Yet, I believe that it developed with the horizons of axial consciousness and represents one of its possible trajectories. In fact, at the same time that science enlarged the understanding of matter, it progressively narrowed Western axial consciousness by employing exclusively a mechanical model and by limiting human knowledge to what can be grasped only by an empirical method. In Western science the earlier axial split between matter and spirit was intensified. Descartes ignored spirit and saw mind as a detached observer of mechanical forces. Although this paradigm yielded enormous knowledge of the physical world, its narrow perspective only added to the fragmentation latent in the original axial transformation.

The Second Axial Period

If we shift our gaze from the first millennium BC to the eve of the twenty-first century, we can discern another transformation of consciousness. It is so profound and far-reaching that I call it the Second Axial Period.148 Like the first, it is happening simultaneously around the earth, and, like the first, it will shape the horizon of consciousness for future centuries. Not surprisingly, too, it will have great significance for world religions, which were constituted in the First Axial Period. However, the new form of consciousness is different from that of the First Axial Period. Then it was individual consciousness; now it is global consciousness.

In order to understand better the forces at work in the Second Axial Period, I would like to draw from the thought of paleontologist Pierre Teilhard de Chardin.[160]In light of his research in evolution, he charted the development of consciousness from its roots in the geosphere and biosphere and into the future. In a process that he called "planetization," he observed that a shift in the forces of evolution had occurred over the past century. This shift is from divergence to convergence. When human beings first appeared on this planet, they clustered together in family and tribal units, forming their own group identity and separating themselves from other tribes. In this way humans diverged, creating separate nations and a rich variety of cultures. However, the spherical shape of the earth prevented unlimited divergence. With the increase in population and the rapid development of communication, groups could no longer remain apart. After dominating the process for millennia, the forces of divergence have been superseded by those of convergence. This shift to convergence is drawing the various cultures into a single planetized community. Although we have been conditioned by thousands of years of divergence, we now have no other course open to us but to cooperate creatively with the forces of convergence as these are drawing us toward global consciousness.[160]

According to Teilhard, this new global consciousness would not level all differences among peoples; rather, it would generate what he called creative unions in which diversity is not erased but intensified. His understanding of creative unions was based on his general theory of evolution and the dynamic that he observed throughout the universe. From the geosphere to the biosphere to the realm of consciousness, a single process is at work, which he articulated as the law of "complexity-consciousness" and "union differentiates." "In any domain," he wrote, "whether it be the cells of a body, the members of a society or the elements of a spiritual synthesis—*union differentiates.*"[161] From subatomic particles to global consciousness, individual elements unite in what Teilhard called center-to-center unions. By touching each other at the creative core of their being, they release new energy, which leads to more complex units. Greater complexity leads to greater interiority, which, in turn, leads to more creative unions. Throughout the process, the individual elements do not lose their identity but, rather, deepen and fulfill it through union. "Following the confluent orbits of their centres," he stated, "the grains of consciousness do not tend to lose their outlines and blend, but, on the contrary, to accentuate the depth and incommunicability of their *egos*. The more 'other' they become in conjunction, the more they find themselves as 'self.'"[162] At this point of history, because of the shift from divergence to convergence, the forces of planetization are bringing about an unprecedented complexification of consciousness through the convergence of cultures and religions.

In light of Teilhard's thought, then, we can better understand the meeting of religions on the eve of the twenty-first century. The world religions are the product of the First Axial Period and the forces of divergence. Although in the first millennium BC, there was a common transformation of consciousness, it occurred in diverse geographical regions within already differentiated cultures. In each case the religion was shaped by this differentiation in its origin and developed along differentiated lines. This produced a remarkable richness of spiritual wisdom, of spiritual energies, and of religious-cultural forms to express, preserve, and transmit this heritage. Now that the forces of divergence have shifted to convergence, the religions must meet each other in center-to-center unions, discovering what is most authentic in each other, releasing creative energy toward a more complexified form of religious consciousness.

Such a creative encounter has been called the "dialogic dialogue" to distinguish it from the dialectic dialogue in which one tries to refute the claims of the other.[163] This dialogic dialogue has three phases: (1) The partners meet each other in an atmosphere of mutual understanding, ready to alter misconceptions about each other and eager to appreciate the values of the other. (2) The partners are mutually enriched, by passing over into the consciousness of the other so that each can experience the other's values from within the other's perspective. This can be enormously enriching, for often the partners discover in another tradition values that are submerged or only inchoate in their own. It is important at this point to respect the autonomy of the other tradition: in Teilhard's terms, to achieve union in which differences are valued as a basis of creativity. (3) If such a creative union is achieved, then the religions will have moved into the complexified form of consciousness that will be characteristic of the twenty-first century. This will be complexified global consciousness, not a mere universal, undifferentiated, abstract consciousness. It will be global through the global convergence of cultures and religions and complexified by the dynamics of dialogic dialogue.

This global consciousness, complexified through the meeting of cultures and religions, is only one characteristic of the Second Axial Period. The consciousness of this period is global in another sense, namely, in rediscovering its roots in the earth. At the very moment when the various cultures and religions are meeting each other and creating a new global community, our life on the planet is being threatened. The very tools that we have used to bring about this convergence—industrialization and technology—are undercutting the biological support system that sustains life on our planet. The future of consciousness, even life on the earth, is shrouded in a cloud of uncertainty by the pollution of our environment, the depletion of natural resources, the unjust distribution of wealth, the stockpiling of nuclear weapons. Unless the human community reverses these destructive forces, we may not see the twenty-first century. The human race as a whole—all the diverse cultures and the religions—must face these problems squarely. In this Second Axial Period we must rediscover the dimensions of consciousness of the spirituality of the primal peoples of the pre-Axial Period. As we saw, this consciousness was collective and cosmic, rooted in the earth and the life cycles. We must rapidly appropriate that form of consciousness or perish from the earth. However, I am not suggesting a romantic attempt to live in the past but that the evolution of consciousness proceeds by way of recapitulation.

Having developed self-reflective, analytic, critical consciousness in the First Axial Period, we must now, while retaining these values, reappropriate and integrate into that consciousness the collective and cosmic dimensions of the pre-axial consciousness. We must recapture the unity of tribal consciousness by seeing humanity as a single tribe, and we must see this single tribe related organically to the total cosmos. This means that the consciousness of the twenty-first century will be global from two perspectives: (1) from a horizontal perspective, cultures and religions must meet each other on the surface of the globe, entering into creative encounters that will produce a complexified collective consciousness; (2) from a vertical perspective, they must plunge their roots deep into the earth in order to provide a stable and secure base for future development. This new global consciousness must be organically ecological, supported by structures that will insure justice and peace. The voices of the oppressed must be heard and heeded: the poor, women, and racial and ethnic minorities. These groups, along with the earth itself, can be looked upon as the prophets and teachers of the Second Axial Period. This emerging twofold global consciousness is not only a creative possibility to enhance the twenty-first century; it is an absolute necessity if we are to survive.

The Task of Religions

What does this mean for religions on the eve of the twenty-first century? It means that they have a double task: to enter creatively into the dialogue of religions, and to channel their energies into solving the common human problems that threaten our future on the earth. It means that they must strip away negative and limiting attitudes toward other religions. They must avoid both a narrow fundamentalism and a bland universalism. They must be true to their spiritual heritage, for this is the source of their power and their gift to the world. They must make every effort to ground themselves in their own traditions and at the same time to open themselves to other traditions. In concert with the other religions, they should commit themselves to creating the new complexified global consciousness we have been exploring.

Just to meet, even creatively, on the spiritual level is not enough. They must channel their spiritual resources toward the solution of global problems. For the most part, this calls for a transformation of the religions. Having been formed in the First Axial Period, the religions bear the mark of axial consciousness: in turning toward the spiritual ascent, away from the material. The religions must rediscover the material dimension of existence and its spiritual significance. In this they can learn from the secular that justice and peace are human values that must be cherished and pragmatically cultivated. However, they must not adopt an exclusively secular attitude, for their unique contribution is to tap their reservoirs of spiritual energy and channel this into developing secular enterprises that are genuinely human. It is in this larger context that I believe the religions of the world—must face together the challenges of the Second Axial Period.

ENDNOTES

Introduction

1. Sandra Schneiders, IHM, "Biblical Spirituality: Life, Literature, and Learning" in *Doors of Understanding. Conversations on Global Spirituality in Honor of Ewert Cousins*, ed. Steven L. Chase (Quincy, IL: Franciscan Press, 1997), p. 53.
2. Later published with the same title: *Fires of Desire: Erotic Energies and the Spiritual Quest* eds. Fredrica Halligan and John J. Shea (New York: Crossroad, 1992).
3. Sr. Mary Margaret Funk, OSB "An Interview with Fr. James Wiseman, OSB *Monastic Interreligious Dialogue* Bulletin 83 (July 2009) www.monasticdialog.com.
4. John Dunne *The Way of All the Earth* (Notre Dame: Notre Dame University, 1978), p. ix.
5. Huston Smith "Come Higher, My Friend" in *Doors of Understanding: Conversations on Global Spirituality in Honor of Ewert Cousins*, ed. Steven L. Chase (Quincy, IL: Franciscan Press, 1997), p. 203.
6. Ewert Cousins, unpublished document, 2003.

Chapter 1

7. H. Coventry, *Philemon*, Conv. I, II, 59, cited in *The Oxford English Dictionary*, s.v. "Mysticism."
8. Augustine, *Confessions*, VII, 10; the English translations of Augustine are taken from *The Confessions of St. Augustine*, trans. Rex Warner (New York: New American Library, 1963).
9. Ibid.
10. Ibid.; the italicized words are from Scripture: Rom. 1:20.
11. Ibid., 17.
12. Ibid., 10.
13. Ibid., 17.
14. Ibid., VIII, 1.
15. Ibid., 12; Rom., 13:13.
16. Ibid., IX, 10.
171. Bonaventure, *Itinerarium*, I, 9; the English translations of this work are my own, taken from Bonaventure: *The Soul's Journey into God, The Tree of life, The Life of St. Francis.* (New York: Paulist Press, 1978).
18. Ibid., II, 8.
19. Ibid., III, 4.
20. Ibid., IV, 1, 2.
21. Ibid., V, 6. Deut. 6:4.
22. Ibid., VI, 2.
23. Ibid., 4, 6: Isa. 13:9.

Chapter 2

24. Dante, *Paradiso*, xxxiii, 1. 145.

25. Richard Payne, "A Mystical Body of Love" (paper delivered at the interreligious dialogue conference on the theme *The Spirituality of Love in the Twelfth Century and Today*, held at Nantes, France, June 1-4, 1986).

26. Origen, *Commentary on the Song of Songs*, prologue; English translation by Roland Greer, *Origen: An Exhortation to Martyrdom, Prayer, and Selected Works*, *The Classics of Western Spirituality* (New York: Paulist Press, 1979), p. 217.

Chapter 3

27. Cf. Robert McNally, *The Unreformed Church* (New York: Sheed and Ward, 1965), pp. 148-86; Jean Leclercq, Francois Vandenbroucke, [and] Louis Bouyer, *The Spirituality of the Middle Ages*, trans. the Benedictines of Holme Eden Abbey, Carlisle (New York: Desclee, 1968), pp. 243-50; Gabriel Braso, *Liturgy and Spirituality* (Collegeville, MN: Liturgical Press, 1960), pp. 30-55.

28. Cf. the commentary in *The Jerusalem Bible* (Garden City: Doubleday, 1966), p. 315.

29. Cf. Jean Leclercq, *The Love of Learning and the Desire for God*, trans. Catharine Misrahi (New York: Fordham University Press, 1974), pp. 88-90.

30. *Bernard of Clairvaux*, In Cant. 20.6, trans. Kilian Walsh *Song of Songs I* (Kalamazoo: Cistercian Publications, 1979), p. 152.

31. Bonaventure, *Legenda maior*. III. 1, trans. Ewert Cousins, *The Soul's Journey into God, The Tree of Life, The Life of St. Francis* (New York, Paulist Press, 1978), p. 199. Cf. also Thomas of Celano, *Vita prima*, 22.

32. Ibid. III, 3; Cousins, p. 201.

33. Thomas of Celano, *Vita prima*. 84, trans. Placid Hermann, *St. Francis of Assisi: First and Second Life of St. Francis* (Chicago: Franciscan Herald Press, 1963), p. 76.

34. Ibid., 85-86, trans., 76-77.

35. *Brevarium Romanum, Officium nativitatis Domini*, noc. 1, resp. 2.

36. Bonaventure, *Lignum vitae*, 4, see my trans. note 5, *The Tree of Life* pp. 128-29.

37. Ignatius of Loyola, *Spiritual Exercises*, trans. Anthony Mattola, *The Spiritual Exercises of St. Ignatius* (Garden City: Image Book, 1964), pp. 70-71.

38. Ibid., trans, p. 71.

39. Ewert Cousins, "Francis of Assisi: Christian Mysticism at the Crossroads," in *Mysticism and Religious Traditions*, Steven T. Katz, ed. (New York: Oxford University Press, 1983).

40. Bonaventure, *Itinerarium mentis in Deum*. prol., 3, see my trans. note 5, *The Soul's Journey Into God*, p. 55.

41. Ibid., VI, 2. see my trans. note 5, *The Soul's Journey Into God,* p. 103.

Chapter 5

42. Mircea Eliade, *Patterns in Comparative Religion*, trans. Rosemary Sheed (New York: Sheed and Ward, 1958), p. 29.

43. In approaching this question through the concept of model, we are following a trend in various fields at the present time, e.g., the physical and the social sciences and theology. Cf. Max Black, *Models and Metaphysics* (Ithaca, N.Y.: Cornell University Press, 1962); B. H. Kazemier and D. Vuysje (eds) *The Concept and the Role of the Model in Mathematics and Natural and Social Sciences* (Dordrecht, The Netherlands: Reidel, 1961); Ian Ramsey, *Models and Mystery* (London: Oxford University Press, 1964).

44. Cf. Nicholas of Cusa, *De Docta Ignorantia,* in *Nicolai de Cusa Opera Omnia*, ed. Ernst Hoffmann and Raymond Klibansky (Leipzig: Meiner, 1932).

45. Bonaventure, *Hexaemeron*, coll. 1, in *Doctoris Seraphici S. Bonaventurae Opera Omnia*, 10 vols. (Quaracchi, 1882-1902), V, 329-35. We will use the above text, but will cite the parallel passages in the Delorme text: *S. Bonaventurae Collationes in Hexaemeron et Bonaventuriana Quaedam Selecta*, ed. F. Delorme, O.F.M. (Quaracchi, 1934).

46. Cf. our study of the *coincidentia oppositorum* in the *Itinerarium*: "The Coincidence of Opposites in the Christology of Bonaventure," paper given at the *Conference on Medieval Studies*, the Medieval Institute of Western Michigan University, March 13-15, 1968*; Franciscan Studies* 28 (1968) pp. 27-45.

47. *Itinerarium*, c. 5, n. 7 (V, 309).

48. Ibid., c. 6, n. 3 (V, 311).

49. Ibid., n. 5-6 (V, 311-12).

50. Ibid., n. 7, (V, 312).

51. Ibid., c. 7, n. 1 (V, 312).

52. *Hexaemeron*, coll. 1, n. 11 (V, 331); Delorme, p. 5.

53. Ibid., n. 14 (V, 331-32); Delorme, p. 6. "This must necessarily be the center of the persons: for if there is a person who produces and is not produced and a person who is produced and does not produce, there must necessarily be a central person who is produced and produces."

54. Cf. *Itinerarium*, c. 6, n. 2 (V, 310-11); *I Sent.*, d. 27 (I, 464-92); d. 31, p. 2 (I, 538-52).

55. *Hexaemeron*, coll. 1, n. 13 (V, 331); Delorme, p. 7. "For the Father from eternity generated the Son, similar to himself; and he expressed himself and his own likeness, similar to himself; and in so doing he expressed all his power. He expressed what he could do and especially what he willed to do; and he expressed all things in him, that is, in the Son or in that very center as in his art."

56. Ibid.

57. Ibid.

58. Jo. 16:28: *Hexaemeron*, coll. 1, n. 17 (V, 332); Delorme, p. 7.

59. Ibid. "Lord, I have gone forth from you, who are supreme; I come to you, who are supreme, and through you, who are supreme. This is the metaphysical center that leads us back, and this is our whole metaphysics: emanation, exemplarity

and consummation; that is, to be illumined by spiritual rays and to be led back to the supreme height. Thus you will be a true metaphysician."

60. Ibid., n. 13 (V, 331); Delorme, p. 6; Augustine, *In Epist. Ioannis*, tr. 3, n. 13. "Therefore that center is truth; and it is established according to Augustine and other saints that "Christ, having his chair in heaven, teaches inwardly"; nor can any truth be known in any way except through that truth."

61. *Christus, Unus Omnium Magister*, n. 9 (V, 559).

62. Cf. *III Sent.*, d. 2, a. 1, q. 2, concl. (III, 40).

63. Cf. *De Reductione Artium ad Theologiam*, n. 20 (V, 324).

64. *Hexaemeron*, coll. 1, n. 18-20 (V, 332-33); Delorme, p. 7-10.

65. Phil. 2:5-12.

66. *Hexaemeron*, coll. 1, n. 21-22 (V, 333); Delorme, p. 10.

67. Ibid., n. 24 (V, 333); Delorme, pp. 11. "For when the center of a circle has been lost, it can be found only by two lines intersecting at right angles."

68. Ibid., n. 25-30 (V, 333-34); Delorme, pp. 12-15.

69. Ibid., n. 28 (V, 334); Delorme, pp. 14-15. "The major proposition was from eternity, the minor on the cross and the conclusion in the resurrection. The Jews believed they had confounded Christ, and they taunted him: "If you are the Son of God, come down from the cross" (Mt. 27:40). Now Christ did not say: Let me live. Rather he said: Let me assume death and be linked with the other extreme, to suffer and to die. And then the conclusion follows. And so he tricked the devil."

70. Ibid., n. 31-33 (V, 334-35); Delorme, pp.15-17.

71. Ibid., n. 34-36 (V, 335); Delorme, pp. 17-18.

72. Ibid., n. 37-38 (V, 335); Delorme, p. 18.

73. Cf. n. 1, above.

74. Eliade, op. cit.; cf. also by Eliade, *The Sacred and the Profane*, tr. Willard R. Trask (New York: Harcourt, Brace, 1959); and *The Myth of the Eternal Return*, tr. Willard R. Trask (New York: Pantheon, 1954). Cf. C. G. Jung, *The Collected Works of C. G. Jung*, tr. R. F. C. Hull (New York: Pantheon, 1953-).

75. Eliade, *The Sacred and the Profane*, pp. 36-37.

76. Jolande Jacobi, *The Psychology of C.G. Jung*, tr. Ralph Manheim (New Haven: Yale University, 1962), pp. 131-32.

77. *Itinerarium,* prol., n. 2 (V, 295); c. 6, n. 4 (V, 311); c. 7, n. 1 (V, 312). An extended study of the symbols of the *Itinerarium* from the standpoint of Eliade's research has been made by Sister Lillian Turney, C.D.P.: "The Symbolism of the Temple in St. Bonaventure's *Itinerarium Mentis in Deum*," unpublished doctoral dissertation (New York: Fordham University, Department of Theology, 1968).

Chapter 6

78. Bonaventure, *Legenda maior*, II, 4. All English translations of Bonaventure are taken from *Bonaventure: The Soul's Journey into God, The Tree of Life, The Life of St. Francis*, trans. Ewert Cousins (New York: Paulist Press, 1978).

79. Ibid.
80. Ibid.
81. Ibid., XIV, 3-4.
82. Thomas of Celano, *Vita prima*, 7.
83. Sacrum Commercium, 1-13.
84. Dante, *La Divina commedia, Paradiso*, XI, 70-73.
85. Bonaventure, *Legenda maior*, II, 1.
86. *Legenda Perugina*, 43; English translation by Rosalind Brooke, *Scripta Leonis, Rufini et Angeli Sociarum S. Francisci* (Oxford: Clarendon, 1970).
87. Ibid.
88. Ibid.
89. Ibid.
90. Ibid.
91. The Umbrian text of the canticle is from the critical edition of Kajetan Esser, OFM, *Opuscula Sancti Francisci_*(Grottaferrata: Editiones Collegie S. Bonaventurae, 1978), pp. 84-85. The English translation is my own from the volume cited in note 1 above, pp. 27-28.
92. See Bonaventure, *Itinerarium mentis in Deum.*
93. See my treatment of this in *Global Spirituality: Towards the Meeting of Mystical Paths* (Madras: University of Madras, 1978).
94. *Sacrum Commercium*, 63.
95. Bonaventure, *Legenda maior*, XIII, 3.
96. Bonaventure, *Itinerarium*, VII, 6.
97. Bonaventure, *Legenda maior*, XIII, 3.
98. See my development of this theme in *Bonaventure and the Coincidence of Opposites* (Chicago: Franciscan Herald Press, 1978).
99. Bonaventure, *Itinerarium*, prologue, 1.

Chapter 7
100. Rudolf Otto, *Mysticism East and West* (New York: Macmillan 1960).
101. A further development of these lectures has since appeared in a book: *Global Spirituality: Toward the Meeting of Mystical Paths* (Madras: University of Madras, 1985).
102. Rudolf Otto, *The Idea of the Holy* (New York: Oxford University Press, 1958).
103. Steven Katz, "Language, Epistemology and Mysticism," in *Mysticism and Philosophical Analysis*, Steven Katz, ed. (New York: Oxford University Press, 1978), pp. 22-74.
104. Eckhart, *German Works: Sermon 52*, trans. Edmund Colledge, in *Meister Eckhart: The Essential Sermons, Commentaries, Treatises, and Defense*, Edmund Colledge and Bernard McGinn, eds. *Classics of Western Spirituality* (New York: Paulist Press, 1981), pp. 199-200.
105. Eckhart, 200.
106. Eckhart, Sermon 48, 198.
107. Eckhart, Sermon 83, 206.

108. For a treatment of this notion of the coincidence of opposites, see my *Bonaventure and the Coincidence of Opposites* (Chicago: Franciscan Herald Press, 1978) and "Fullness and Emptiness in Bonaventure and Eckhart," *Dharma*, 6 (1981): pp. 59-68.

Chapter 8

109. See my article "Spirituality in Today's World," in *Religion in Today's World: The Religious Situation of the World From 1945 to the Present Day*, Frank Whaling, ed. (Edinburgh: T. & T. Clark, 1987), pp. 306-34.

110. See the series *World Spirituality*, cited in note 4, below.

111. See "Spirituality in Today's World."

112. To date nine volumes have appeared: *Christian Spirituality*, vol. 1 ed. Bernard McGinn, John Meyendorff, and Jean LeClerq, vol. 2 ed. Jill Raitt in collaboration with Bernard McGinn and Jean Meyendorff, and vol. 3 ed. Louis Dupré and Don E. Saliers in collaboration with John Meyendorff; *Jewish Spirituality*, vols. 1 and 2 ed. Arthur Green; *Islamic Spirituality*, vols. 1 and 2 ed. Seyyed Hossein Nasr; *Hindu Spirituality*, vol. 1, ed. Krishna Sivaraman; and *Classical Mediterranean Spirituality* ed. A. H. Armstrong.

113. Quoted in the preface to each volume in the series *World Spirituality: An Encyclopedic History of the Religious Quest* (New York: Crossroad.

114. Augustine, *Confessions*, I, 1.

115. Ibid., VII, 10.

116. Bernard de Clairvaux, *Sermons on the Song of Songs*, VII, 2.

117. Bonaventure, *The Soul's Journey into God*, prologue, 3.

1180. Ibid., VII, 6.

119. Teresa of Avila, *The Interior Castle*, I, 1.

120. Ibid., VII, 6.

121. C.G. Jung, *Memories, Dreams, Reflections* (New York: Pantheon Books, 1963), pp. 158-59.

122. R.E.L. Masters and Jean Houston, *The Varieties of Psychedelic Experience* (New York: Holt, Rinehart, and Winston, 1966).

123. Ibid., p. 181.

124. Stanislav Grof, *Realms of the Human Unconscious* (New York: Viking Press, 1975), p. 42.

125. Ibid, pp. 40-41.

126. Masters and Houston, *Varieties of Psychedelic Experience*, p. 207.

127. Grof, *The Realms of the Human Unconscious,* p. 45.

128. Masters and Houston, *Varieties of Psychedelic Experience*, pp. 218-19.

129. Grof, *The Realms of the Human Unconscious*, p. 147

130. Ibid.

131. Masters and Houston, *Varieties of Psychedelic Experience*, p. 308.

132. Karl Jaspers, *The Origin and Goal of History*, trans. Michael Bullock (New Haven: Yale University Press, 1953), p. 1.

133. Revisions in the chronology of the development of Zoroastrianism indicate a date for Zoroaster c. 1800 BC rather than c. 800 BC. Ed.

Chapter 9

134. Jean Leclercq presented this position in a public lecture at Fordham University, New York, November 30, 1976; cf. my summary of his position in my article "Raimundo Panikkar and the Christian Systematic Theology of the Future" Cross Currents 29 (Summer 1979), pp. 141-155.

135. Cf. Pierre Teilhard de Chardin, Le phénomène humain (Paris: Editions du Seuil, 1955), pp. 263-278.

136. For data on the dialogue of world religions, cf. the Bulletin of the Vatican Secretariat for Non-Christians, 1966; also the publications of the World Council of Churches, for example, Towards World Community: The Colombo Papers, S.J. Samartha, ed., (Geneva, WCC, 1975); Living Faiths and Ultimate Goals, S.J. Samartha, ed. (Geneva, WCC, 1974); Christian-Muslim Dialogue, S.J. Samartha and J.B. Taylor, eds., (Geneva: WCC, 1973).

137. Raimundo Panikkar, Myth, Faith and Hermeneutics: Cross Cultural Studies (New York: Paulist Press, 1979).

138. Cf. especially "La pluralisation de l'herméneutique: la metamorphose de la philosophie de la religion," in L'Herméneutique de la philosophie de la religion, ed. Enrico Castelli (Paris: Aubier, 1977), pp. 205-217.

139. William James, The Varieties of Religious Experience (New York: Longmans, Green and Co., 1902; cf. also R.E.L. Masters and Jean Houston, The Varieties of Psychedelic Experience (New York: Holt, Rinehart and Winston, 1966).

140. Cf. my article "Les forms nouvelles du Sacré aux Etats-Unis" in Prospective sul Sacro, ed. Enrico Castelli (Roma: Istituto di Studi Filosofici, 1974), pp. 205-223.

141. On the notion of the person as image of the Trinity, cf. Augustinem De Trinitate, VIII-XV.

142. For a medieval example of this method cf. Bonaventure, De reduction atrium ad theologiam.

143. For a further treatment of this matter cf. my article referred to in note 5, above.

144. Cf. my article "Raimundo Panikkar and the Christian Systematic Theology of the Future," cited in note 1, above.

Chapter 10

145. John Dunne, *The Way of All the Earth* (Notre Dame: Notre Dame University, 1978), ix.

146. Ervin Laszlo, *Science and the Akashic Field: An Integral Theory of Everything* (Rochester, VT: Inner Traditions, 2004).

147. See the first installment of this article in *MID Bulletin*, Issue 73, section on "Conference at the United Nations: October 24, 1975."

148. Pierre Teilhard de Chardin, *Le Phénomène humain* (Paris: Éditions du Seuil, 1955), pp. 268-269.

149. Ibid., p. 292. English translation by Bernard Wall, *The Phenomenon of Man* (New York: Harper & Row, 1965), p. 262.

150. Ibid.

151. Ibid., p. 335; in translation, p. 302.

152.   Karl Jaspers, *Vom Ursprung und Ziel der Geschichte* (Zürich: Artemis, 1949), pp. 19-43.

153.   Ibid. p. 19; English translation by Michael Bullock, *The Origin and Goal of History* (New Haven: Yale University Press, 1953), p. 1.

154.   Although the series was planned to contain 60 volumes, it has been transformed into an open-ended series with all titles kept in print. The present number of volumes is 111.

155.   Ewert Cousins, *Global Spirituality: Toward the Meeting of Mystical Paths.* Developed from a series of five special lectures delivered at the Radhakrishnan Institue for Advanced Study in Philosophy at the University of Madras, India, January 18-24, 1984. Madras: University of Madras, 1985.

156.   Robley Edward Whitson, *The Coming Convergence of World Religions* (New York: Newman Press, 1971), p. x.

Chapter 12

157.   Karl Jaspers, *Vom Ursprung und Ziel der Geschichte* (Zurich: Artemis, 1949), pp. 19–43.

158.   Ibid., p. 19; E.T.: *The Origin and Goal of History*, tr. Michael Bullock (New Haven, CT: Yale University Press, 1953), p. 1. For the ongoing academic discussion of Jaspers' position on the Axial Period, see "Wisdom, Revelation, and Doubt: Perspectives on the First Millennium B.C.," *Daedalus* 104 (Spring, 1975): v–vi, 1–172; and S. N. Eisenstadt, ed., *The Origins and Diversity of Axial Age Civilizations*, SUNY Near Eastern Studies (Albany, NY: State University of New York Press, 1986).

159.   For a more comprehensive treatment of my concept of the Second Axial Period, see my *Christ of the 21st Century* (Rockport, MA: Element, 1992; New York: Continuum, 1992).

160.   Pierre Teilhard de Chardin, *Le Phénomène humain* (Paris: Editions du Seuil, 1955); see also idem, *L'Activation de l'énergie* (Paris: Editions du Seuil, 1962), and idem, *L'Energie humaine* (Paris: Editions du Seuil, 1962). For a more detailed study of Teilhard's thought in relation to the Second Axial Period, see my paper, "Teilhard de Chardin and the Religious Phenomenon," delivered in Paris at the International Symposium on the Occasion of the Centenary of the Birth of Teilhard de Chardin, organized by UNESCO, September 16–18, 1981, UNESCO Document Code: SS.82/WS/36.

161.   Teilhard, *Le Phénomène humain*, pp. 268–269.

162.   Ibid., p. 292; E.T.: *The Phenomenon of Man,* tr. Bernard Wall (New York: Harper and Row, 1959; 2nd ed., 1965), p. 262.

163.   Ibid. (his emphasis).

164.   On the concept of dialogic dialogue, see Raimundo Panikkar, *Myth, Faith, and Hermeneutics* (New York: Paulist Press, 1979), pp. 241–245; also see idem, *The Intrareligious Dialogue* (New York: Paulist Press, 1978).

About the Author

Ewert H. Cousins was born June 23, 1927 in New Orleans. At age eighteen he joined the Society of Jesus, and later left, completing his Ph.D. in philosophy at Fordham. He taught in the Theology Department, becoming Professor Emeritus after 40 years at Fordham.

He became a "world-renowned theologian and pioneer in interreligious dialogue who brought Christians, Hindus, Muslims Jews and Buddhists together at gatherings around the globe, from the United Nations to the University of Madras."[1]

Cousins was the General Editor of the 25 volume series *World Spirituality: An Encyclopedic History of the Religious Quest* and the Editorial Consultant of the series *Classics of Western Spirituality*. He was a translator of Bonaventure, and author of numerous books including *Christ of the 21st Century, Bonaventure and the Coincidence of Opposites*, and *Global Spirituality: Toward the Meeting of Mystical Paths* and editor of *Hope and the Future of Man* and *Process Theology*. .

A past president of the American Teilhard Association, he was a consultant to the Pontifical Council for Interreligious Dialogue, and a member of the Advisory Board for Monastic Interreligious Dialogue.

In 1964 he was an early participant in the Easter Week seminars of the United Institute which subsequently evolved into the programs of the Graduate Theological Foundation. He was among the initial faculty members of the doctoral programs of the Foundation. In 1980 he was named the Teilhard de Chardin Professor of Christian Spirituality at the Foundation. He died on May 30, 2009.

Emily Cousins, Obituary in the *Republican-American* Thursday, June 4th, 2009.

Made in the USA
Monee, IL
09 July 2021

73282012R00090